W9-DCH-593

WHAT MEN NEED TO KNOW

About Women

DENNIS LEONARD

LEGACY PUBLISHERS INTERNATIONAL
DENVER, COLORADO

WHAT MEN NEED TO KNOW ABOUT WOMEN

ISBN 1-880809-51-6

Printed in the United States of America

Copyright © 2006 - by Legacy Publishers International

Legacy Publishers International
1301 South Clinton Street
Denver, CO 80247
Phone: 303-283-7480
FAX: 303-283-7536
www.legacypublishersinternational.com

Library of Congress Cataloging-in-Publication data Pending

Printed in the United States of America

1 2 3 4 5 6 7 8 9 10 11 12 13 / 13 12 11 10 09 08 07 06

TABLE OF CONTENTS

INTRODUCTION

I n the last century, mankind has accomplished some amazing things. We have gone from mastering flight to putting a man on the moon, split the atom, decoded the genome, created the computer, and broken the sound barrier. Why is it then that the most important thing of all, our ability to find a mate to build a happy future and family together with, still remains such a baffling mystery?

Over the years, however, as a businessman, husband, and now pastor, I have found that while all women are unique and each must be dealt with in her own special way, there are some overall keys that can help men more successfully reach across the gender gap to build joyful relationships that can last a lifetime.

In the following pages, you will not only uncover eleven important keys to making this a reality in your life, but also come to understand them in a way that will make them real and practical in your life. Believe it or not, I have found the women in our lives—especially the one woman we want to spend the rest of our life with—are a mystery worth pursuing. While they are also a mystery we may never fully understand, the joy is often more in the pursuit than in the discoveries made along the way.

There are a lot of different theories about how to get the most out of life and our relationships with women. The keys I subscribe here are for the long-term, not the short-term—they are about quality, not quantity. Look at where you want to be with the woman of your dreams not only before the end of the evening, but also in the next ten, twenty, and even fifty years of your life.

My hope is that with the keys in this book, your life will reflect all the joy and fulfillment possible with the woman of your dreams.

Here's to a little heaven on earth for all of us!

Dennis Leonard
Denver, Colorado

Chapter One

THE BATTLE OF THE SEXES... TWENTY-FIRST CENTURY STYLE

———⟫⟩•⟨⟪———

Nobody will ever win the battle of the sexes. There's too much fraternizing with the enemy.

Henry Kissinger

A lot of people in recent decades have tried to down play the differences between men and women. For those people, I have a few things they should consider: toilet seats, sports, hunting, shopping, and what the proper use of a remote control is.

Mull over some of the following paradoxes and see if you understand what I am getting at:

1) Women like to discuss problems, but don't want help finding solutions.

2) Women always worry about the things that men forget; men always worry about the things women remember.

3) Women expect their men to "just know" why they are crying, when the other half of the time they complain we don't understand them even when we do talk together.

4) Men are known for being more analytical, yet using something other than their brain to think with most of the time.

5) Women can go on a shopping spree and come home to talk about nothing but how much money she saved.

6) Women are accused of being poor drivers, but do most of the chauffeuring of America's youth.

7) Anything you say can and will be used against you. (Okay, that doesn't sound like a paradox, but how often have you tried to say something nice only to have it used against you later? That's a paradox!)

8) Men communicate best when they don't talk.

9) A woman can't remember where she put her car keys, but can remember everything you have ever said about her mother.

10) When a woman starts a sentence with "Now tell me the truth," that is the last thing in the world you should probably do.

In the famous words from Cool Hand Luke, "What we have here is failure to communicate."

Face it: men and women aren't just different physically, but in how we think, approach issues, experience emotions, and relate to others. As author John Gray,

Ph.D. put it, it's as if we are from different planets, but we have just forgotten.

DIFFERENT PLANETS, DIFFERENT WORLDS

The premise of Dr. Gray's book, *Men Are from Mars, Women Are from Venus,* is that seemingly men and women are indeed from different planets, and though they may have traveled to earth together, they have since developed selective amnesia. We have never changed who we are in essence, but we have forgotten that we are from different worlds and now can't figure out why we have such a problem communicating and getting along. The problem is, because we think differently, see the world differently, have different expectations, and tend to mean different things even though we use the same words, we have tremendous misunderstandings that can escalate as far as total nuclear family meltdown.

~

There are two times when a man doesn't understand a woman—before marriage
and after marriage.
Anonymous

~

As the traditional roles of women began to change after World War II, it was as if everything we had known about the sexes before was thrown into question and we needed to sort it all out again. It appeared that women could do pretty much anything that men could do—and often do it better—and that men could do almost everything women could do—except have babies. Women erupted into the workforce to throw their shoulders to the wheel of commerce. As a result, the 1980s and 1990s have been the most prosperous times the world has ever known.

At the dawn of the twenty-first century, women are now a mainstay of our national workforce and there is no place, including the military, where they are not in there right beside the men who were doing it all alone just half a century ago. Women run corporations, teach in universities, perform surgeries, fight wars, negotiate treaties, lead countries, and do basically everything only men used to do, and in a lot of ways, on the whole, the world seems a better place for it.

However, there is just one problem. Even after the additional time we are spending together because women are now both in the workplace and at home, current divorce rates indicate that men and women seem to be getting along worse than they ever have before. In a time and culture where individuals are more and more isolated, such an inability to get along has become catastrophic to our families and communities.

While there were some things about the women's liberation movement and the sexual revolution of the 1960s and 1970s that were good, there have been a lot of things that have gotten messed up as well. One notion that seems to have set us back is perhaps what has caused a bit of our selective amnesia: the idea that men and women could be equal in what they do and therefore—except for a few very noticeable physical attributes—were essentially the same on the inside.

We need to realize that despite cultural changes, men and women have not essentially changed in the way they approach life, think, or relate to others. Understanding a few of these major differences can go a long way in helping us better get along together and find more fulfill-ment in our relationships and lives. And while generaliza-tions between the sexes are never universally true, they are still useful in communicating between male and female/Martian and Venusian cultures. A small fraction of men may identify more with Venusians and a fraction of women may identify more with Martians, but this is not an indication that they are not normal men and women, only that they might have an advantage in understanding the opposite sex. These differences can help us be more open to where others are coming from and ultimately relate better to one another across the gender gap.

~

The difference between men and women is that, if given the choice between saving the life of an infant or catching a fly ball, a woman will automatically choose to save the infant, without even considering if there's a man on base.

Dave Barry

~

The other side of that is, of course, that we men also need to understand our own tendencies and how we relate to others, specifically the women in our lives, so that we can live more happily together with them. Perhaps there is something we can do less or more of to reduce the friction that is driving *us* crazy at the same time it is driving *them* away.

With that said, it is good that we men take time to look at some of the general differences between men and women and see if they don't help us as we try to relate with the fairer sex (and by the way, that is *fairer* as in "better looking", not *fairer* as in "more reasonable", but we will get to that later).

TIM THE TOOL MAN MEETS MARTHA STEWART

Guys, we tend to focus on tasks and solutions, where women tend to focus on people and processes. We focus on accomplishments and what we have done, while women tend to say, "Now, how are we all feeling? Is everyone happy about what we have just accomplished? Does anyone have anything they would like to share with the rest of us?"

> Guys, we tend to focus on tasks and solutions, where women tend to focus on people and processes.

How often has it happened that you and your girlfriend go out after work—or if you are married, you both come home after work—and she starts telling you about her day. After some initial chit chat she launches into a painfully-detailed description of an issue she faced that day or one that has been bugging her for some time. What do you do? The minute you have about two facts, you are already calculating a solution, and, in your brilliance, you cut in to share it with her. What does she do? Is she floored by your astuteness and incredible problem-solving insight? Does she thank you and start gently rubbing her foot on your calf in gratitude and suggest you turn the lights down a bit? Of course not. The general response is something along the line of, "Do you mind? Please don't interrupt when I am trying to tell you something! Just listen!"

When men confront a problem, they need to fix it. When women confront a problem, they want to share how they *feel* about it.

~

On one hand we'll never experience childbirth;
on the other we can open our own jars.
Bruce Willis

~

If you have ever watched *Home Improvement* you will remember scenes where Tim rushes in to fix something before he has all the information and the results are disastrous—and I am talking about a relationship issue with his family, not something where he ends up in the emergency room (though I think he still ended up in the emergency room after several of those as well!). What was his problem? Number 1, his help in solving the problem for his wife was seldom actually requested, and number 2, his bungling and hastiness normally overpowered his wisdom.

As men, we are creatures of action. Women are creatures of contemplation and discussion. Men tend to focus on what needs to be done; women tend to focus on feelings and attitudes. Men tend to care more about getting things done than the morale of the team; women tend to care more about the morale than the tasks at hand. Men manage others like fathers, engendering independence and emphasizing responsibility and competence; women manage like mothers, nurturing for growth and rewarding for how those they supervise improve their environments and engender cooperation.

Men emphasize function, women emphasize form. Just as a bachelor will come home from work, grab some leftover whatever from the refrigerator and sit down in front of the television to eat, a woman will prepare dinner so that it creates an atmosphere for family as well as providing everyone a nutritional meal. Men are just glad they aren't hungry anymore.

> As men, we tend to want to conquer, while women tend to want to nurture.

Men in general are risk takers; women in general are not. Men will do crazy things to accomplish their dreams and goals. Men will go from one city to another for what they see as a better opportunity. They'll sell their house and invest in something. Women need the security of a home and will cling to it. A man can move from house to house and not even think about it. As men, we need to realize that bringing home a paycheck is not all there is to communicating love. We also have to provide a place for our wives to nest and make a home—often a better job for more money doesn't help when it uproots your family from a good neighborhood, good schools, and a great community and church.

These differences can be either assets or liabilities depending on how we use them. If we understand each other and rely on each other's strengths, we can accomplish great things together; if we don't, we can drive each other nuts!

PAC-MAN MEETS TOUR GUIDE BARBIE

As men, we tend to want to conquer, while women tend to want to nurture. Since our creation, men have had an inner drive to subdue the earth and rule over every living creature. That's why we get up so early in the morning to go fishing, and we don't even care really about how we look or even catching any fish! We will go and catch and release just for the thrill of each individual victory. We are out there conquering, and showing the fish who the boss is! And not only that, but we compete with those that went with us for who caught the most or the biggest without even thinking about it.

In the corporate world, we will make deals in exactly the same way. In fact, we will make deals where we lose money sometimes rather than risk defeat! It's not the deal. It's not the money. It's the conquering—the subduing. We went into the situation and convinced the other person to do what we wanted. That is one more victory for us! Mark it up on the scoreboard!

When men get behind the wheel of a car, it's the same. We want to mark off miles the way a school kid marks off days until summer vacation. We turn into Pac-Man, gobbling up the miles on the road like those little dots in the game. How many more can we get before we need to stop again for gas or a restroom break? "Honey, can you wait just one more exit?" That's why we get so upset when a car pulls in front of us. They are interfering with our conquering. Buckle your seatbelt! We're passing this truck! Hang on!

That's also why we're in front of the TV watching that football, basketball, baseball, or hockey game; we and our team are conquering. If there is a prize, a championship, a game to win, or a goal to be scored, we are locked into the thrill of the conquering or the agony of the defeat.

And how about when it comes to shopping? I don't even go with my wife anymore. She doesn't even want me to go. If we go to the mall or something, she'll go inside, and I'll stay out front. She'll be in there watching me through the window saying, "I wish he would sit down," but I can't, I have to go do something else because the way women shop makes no sense to me.

We men shop like hunters and conquerors. We approach it the same way we approach road trips. We take the shortest, fastest route to where we want to go and what we want to get. We go to one store, we walk straight to the section we need, we find what we want, buy it, we throw it over our shoulder, get back in the car, and go home. In about ten minutes we're done! We check it off our list of "Things to Conquer That Day" and on to the next conquest. It's tagged and bagged. Mission accomplished.

Women, on the other hand, go from one shop to another as if they don't even know what they are looking for. They'll try on thirty-two different outfits and not buy one—*not even one.* To men, shopping means buying things; to women, it is more like the Tour Guide Barbie segment in *Toy Story 2.* They are there for the journey and to take in the sites of the merchandise. For women, the joy is not in the capture, but in the journey itself and in the sharing of that journey. That is why women rarely shop alone, and if they do, then they enlist the sales-women in the store to give them their opinions: "I don't know, do you think this goes with my eyes? It doesn't make me look fat, does it?" Unless we need to find some info, men tend to avoid salespeople because they know their purpose is to convince us to buy something; women are ready to put salespeople on their Christmas card lists the minute they leave the store!

This difference is one of the problems we run into with dating and marriage. For guys, the dating is the hunt, the pursuit, and the marriage is the conquest. Take that woman home, carry her over the threshold, and—for all intents and purposes—she's tagged, bagged, and cap-tured—game over.

Yet for the woman, the fun's in the pursuit, not the conquest. So when the man takes her home and then stops pursuing her—uh oh! The trail goes cold. The man shows up to the bedroom expecting to enjoy the reward of his prize bride and it is suddenly, "Not tonight, honey, I have a headache," or "It's too late, I'm tired." Suddenly she is losing interest because there's no chase any more. And we as men are clueless as to what is happening. We love her as much as we did the day we brought her home, but she doesn't feel it because we are no longer pursuing her.

~

A great marriage is not when the "perfect couple" comes together. It is when an imperfect couple learns to enjoy their differences.
Dave Meurer

~

Women can be unhappy in a marriage because of this. Men, we need to learn to listen. We need to continue to woo. We need to learn to communicate. For women, intimacy starts with your helping to make dinner, or cleaning up afterwards *with your wife*. It starts with listening to her problems without needing to solve them. Your wife wants to know that you want to be with her and invest time in her. She wants a soul mate and companion, not a buddy to call up every once in a while to watch the ballgame.

MR. BOTTOM LINE MEETS MS. DETAILS

As men, we tend not to want any more than a 250-word summary of anything we need to hear about—and if we can get it in twenty-five words, so much the better. Our wife starts to tell us something and in less than ten seconds we start getting bored. We are thinking, "What's the point? Get to the point!" and if we don't get that point soon, we start contemplating work that we need to do on our car.

When men speak to women, however, and plainly state an insight that took hours of thought to express so concisely in a "just-the-facts-ma'am" style, then it carries no weight for her. Anything that could be said so quickly could not have been that important. Important issues must be explored in detail before they are really worth much consideration. Where our coworkers might say, "That is so true," our wives say, "That's nice dear." No wonder men often stay late at the office! If we get more positive feedback and affirmation there, then we start unconsciously wanting to be at work more than at home, and we start opening ourselves up to all kinds of relationship problems with our families because we lose touch with them.

> Men are bottom-line oriented. Women want to communicate because they're social.

Men are bottom-line oriented. Women want to communicate because they're social. Men tend to listen only so long before wondering, "What is the bottom line of where you're going with this, baby?" before we begin to tune out. We can listen to ESPN radio, discuss draft choices for the next season, but we can't listen to our wife tell a story about what happened to little Jimmy on the playground today and the conversation that resulted with his teacher for more than five minutes. Why? Because draft choices have to do with the chances of our team conquering next season, even though there is nothing in the world we can do to ensure our team gets the right ones. Meanwhile, though we love our son and he is definitely in our realm of concern, Jimmy's playground problem appears already to have been taken care of, so what is the point of talking about it anymore?

Sometimes my wife has to get in front of me and say, "Excuse me. I'm talking," because she sees my eyes have glazed over and my mind has wandered somewhere else. The worst thing is to take her out to one of those restaurants that have TVs everywhere. It's horrible. In the midst of one of her most passionate stories, I am suddenly caught up in a game between No-Name State and Who's-Ever-Heard-of-It U playing in the Nobody Cares Bowl on one TV and the high school curling championships from Antarctica on another. I might as well have sunglasses on and be asleep for all the interaction she is getting from me.

Guys, we need to realize that when we look at things, we won't necessarily see them the same way the women in our lives do. If a man is going to paint a room, for example, we think of colors like blue or green; women look for colors like sea-mist-at-sunset or autumn-passion. Men think, "Okay, we will paint, get some new furniture, and just for a change of pace we will put the TV over there and the couch right here." Women think, "Now, we need three different sizes, shapes, and shades of pillows; lampshades; and some different vases for over the fireplace; then we can put a new rug here to tie in the colors of the new curtains . . ." and on and on. Then she will have us move the couch around to ten different places before she decides to put it back right where it started. Women will pick a new chair that was on sale just because it looks good in the corner, even though no one could sit in it for more than five minutes without being uncomfortable. Men, on the other hand, will spend $1,000 on an ugly recliner as if they were adding on a new family room to the house, and justify it because they plan to spend that much time in it.

Women are micro-managers. When women look at a problem, they see several facets of it at once and want to point them all out as they discuss it. Men tend to think more linearly and focus on one element at a time: "The first thing I need to do is . . ." They line them all up and then they don't think of the next step until the current one is done. Women see all the steps simultaneously and want to explore each in detail. When they start to convey every facet to consider, we men tend to get that glaze over our eyes as our brains head out for more tranquil waters. We feel that they are being controlling. We want them to tell us what to do and then leave the "how" up to us, otherwise we feel belittled.

Women can seem to nag because they remember everything and live life in a flurry of considering all their "to dos" at once. Men compartmentalize. Women have instant access to everything that needs to be done in the house at the same time, and keep their "Honey-Do" lists prominent in their prefrontal cortexes. That is why a man, whose mind is blank from a day's work, often hears (as he heads towards his favorite chair in front of the TV) something along the line of "Honey, did you get that screen door fixed yet?" before he ever hits the cushions. While he hasn't thought of that screen door for at least a week, somehow it seems to have been at the forefront of her mind every second of the day since she first asked him to look at it, and now that he has some spare time, shouldn't he finally get to it?

This may also be why women seem to use PDA's quite differently than men. They use them to remember phone numbers and find a slot for everything they need to do in the day; men use them just so they can remember where to be next.

This is also why women can stand a houseful of kids all doing different things at the same time. Men, on the other hand, try to coordinate every group into a team with synchronized actions. If it doesn't follow a coordinated master plan, we have a hard time following it. That is another reason we watch team sports and women prefer figure skating—men like to watch a group working together like a machine towards a goal or goal line; they are an army coordinating to conquer. Women like the grace and finesse of figure skaters—they are poise and poetry in motion all by themselves or with their partners. Women appreciate every detail of every move; men wonder, "What's the score again?" Men get bored watching it because the points aren't awarded until the end, and then the one who wins is simply the one who didn't fall down. For us, it is much easier to determine that the team winning is the one who crosses a goal line more often or puts their ball in the goal more successfully. We don't like things based on judging—in fact, we barely tolerate referees and umpires!

THE CAVEMAN MEETS THE SOCIAL COORDINATOR

When men are stressed out, they look for some place to hide; when women are stressed they reach for the phone or meet a group of friends for coffee. When both get together after a stressful day, it can be like the same poles of a magnet coming together: the more a woman reaches out toward the man, the faster he is repelled away. He is looking for a place to zone out and escape; she is trying to engage.

Men have a tendency to "bury" problems in their brains, pushing them just below the surface of their con-sciousness. They do this while immersing themselves in something more tangibly solvable like watching sports—where they know there will be a resolution to the game before the end of the evening—or playing a video game. Some men tinker in the garage, yard, or around the house for the same reason. All the while they are tackling these more immediate problems before them with about ten percent of their brain, the other ninety percent of their brain is still at the office, plowing through issues raised that day or that week, looking for solutions in unconven-tional—virtually unconscious—ways. Men seek to dis-tract and disengage most of their minds so that this underground work can be done, then when they have found their solution, they reemerge like a conquering hero returning from battle in a far away land.

~

Nevertheless, let every one of you in particular so
love his wife even as himself, and the wife see that
she reverence her husband.
Ephesians 5:33

~

Every time I finish a book that is exactly how I feel; it is like a great weight has lifted and I have come out of a cloud. The world around me is fresh and new and my wife has a hard time figuring out why I am so open and conversational again while for the last several weeks I have been walking around in my thoughts.

Women do a similar thing with their minds, but instead of engaging with mundane tasks or games, they engage in chatter. While they absorb themselves in another person, their sense of worth increases through their interactions—just as a man's does through tasks accomplished (whether they are in real life or some game)—and that positive energy is sent to solving the issues being worked out in their brains.

This difference in approaches can lead to a lot of misunderstandings and hurt feelings if they are misread, which is easily done. Women can feel that men don't care about them anymore or that they are being ignored because all the man does is pull away and want to hide in his "den," whether that is an actual physical room, the back yard, or a recliner in front of the television. Men can also go into their "den" and forget to ever come out, even after their problems are solved, making these feelings of neglect all the stronger for both wives and children. Or, while our wives are talking, we go into the same mode of five to ten percent attention to the world around us while the rest of our brain is elsewhere solving problems. That's the point at which that glaze comes over our eyes. Our wives may even say, "You haven't even been listening," and we respond, "Sure, I was. You said . . ." and repeat a wonderful summary of the last half hour. But the truth is she was right. The tape recorder was on, but you haven't heard a word she said from about ten minutes into the conversation.

In my house, I'm the one who gets up first every morning. So I get up and make the coffee. When my wife gets up, she goes and gets her coffee, comes into my office (we both have offices in our home), and sits down. For the last eight or so hours, she hasn't spoken a word, so now she has to break her communication "fast" no matter what I might be in the middle of. She just begins to talk and she gets it all out. I have to be honest, sometimes I'm listening and sometimes I pretend like I'm listening. Every once in awhile she'll catch me at it and she'll say, "Are you listening?" And I'll go, "Yeah. Yeah." And I can repeat everything she just said, but I have to really concentrate to truly listen.

LAUGHING OR CRYING?

My hope is to present these things in a light-hearted way, but I know some of you who are reading this are realizing these differences could be behind what is happening in your marriage, why your fiancé broke off the engagement, or why the woman who is your immediate supervisor at work drives you crazy. Men and women are just different, and without understanding these differences and adjusting ourselves a bit so that our styles won't clash, we are headed for some major misunderstandings.

We need to let women know that we are not disinterested when we pull away; we are just working something through. We also need to stay focused when she speaks to us so that we don't wander off into the cave of our minds while she is talking—we need to earnestly listen. We need to understand that when she drops her "Honey-Do" list in our laps the minute we sink into our recliners in the evening that she is not trying to nag, but that is just the way her attention span works. She needs to understand that list will be better received if she waits until after the news or we have leafed through the paper before she gives it to us. We also need to realize that watching CNN until midnight or reading the paper until the game starts in order to avoid that list, is no way to let our wives know that we love them.

> We need to let women know that we are not disinterested when we pull away; we are just working something through.

Key #1
Women Are Different Than Men—
But, *Vive la Difference!*
Oh, What Fun Those Differences Can Be!

In essence, all of this requires some understanding, tolerance, communication, and aggressive good will. It takes some insight into who we are as men and some significant study of who are wives are as women—a topic, I admit, that can be incredibly enjoyable if studied in detail.

Chapter Two

NO MAN IS AN ISLAND: BUT IT'S STILL GOOD TO KNOW HOW TO LIVE ON ONE!

There is no fear in love; but perfect love casteth out fear, because fear hath torment. He that feareth is not made perfect in love

1 John 4:18

I don't know if you had the same reaction I did when watching Tom Hanks in *Cast Away*, but I got bored. I mean, I really felt his pain of being trapped all alone on that island for four years. I always liked the part in *Robinson Crusoe* where he was building his house and creating all of those tools and inventions so that he could survive, but it never got very exciting until he met Friday and they had to defend his home from natives or pirates or something. As for Tom, it was interesting how he used those skates and videotapes, but I also understood why they jumped from scenes of his first few weeks, and instead of taking it in smaller increments moved straight to four years later to just before he built his raft. Too much of a man alone is really too much to take. No wonder he seemed to start losing his mind. Just him and Wilson—the volleyball he had painted a face on to keep him company—trying to make the best of things and fighting like a married couple. Wilson was no Friday, and watching a man being stranded alone for four years isn't really entertainment for anyone. Man simply does not do well all alone.

DATING, LONELINESS, AND THE SINGLE GUY

As men, in general, like the first part of *Robinson Crusoe*, being alone is not so bad to us really, as long as we have something to do. In fact, being alone is better for men than it is for women. We like the opportunity to get away and be quiet. We can sit for hours watching a float bob in the water hoping for a fish to bite, or sit in a duck blind in the cold early hours of the morning waiting for something to shoot down. If nothing comes, however, we still endure. It is part of the ritual. For many of us it is the only time in our lives we exhibit real patience. We languish in the outdoors, deep in our thoughts, and consumed by the task before us. Overall it can be relaxing and therapeutic to get away, get alone, and be quiet for a time, but it's no way to live one's life. After a few days, or even a few hours, we are ready for something else. We are hungry to connect with another human being. And there's the rub.

We like being alone, but no one likes being lonely.

No Man Is an Island . . .
But It's Still Good to Know How to Live on One!

In the old war movies like *The Great Escape* or *The Bridge over the River Kwai*, prisoners were disciplined by being locked up in solitary. This still happens today. It was found centuries ago that the easiest way to break a man down was to confine him all by himself. Isolation does crazy things to people. I was always amazed when some of the guys in those old movies came out of the hot boxes like they had been tortured to the edge of endurance, barely able to stand, and stuttering to themselves insanely. Being forced to be alone obviously isn't always a rewarding experience.

GEARED TO BE TOGETHER

In 2003, the Institute for American Values released a study in cooperation with Dartmouth Medical School and the YMCA called *Hardwired to Connect*. The study looked at data on everything from the number of people waiting to see psychology professionals to why people go bowling alone, to how the nurturing characteristics of rats and rhesus monkey parents carry on to their offspring and their offspring's offspring.

That's right! Just as the title indicates, people need to be able to truly connect with other people regularly to be healthy, or more specifically, as the study put it: "we are hardwired for close attachments to other people, beginning with our parents, fathers, extended family, and then moving out to the broader community."

~

Fulfill ye my joy, that ye be likeminded,
having the same love, being of one accord
and of one mind.
Philippians 2:2

~

In other words, lonely kids don't grow up as physically, emotionally, spiritually, and mentally healthy as kids who grow up with strong connections to people who love them. If you grew up in a dysfunctional family—and who didn't—then you will probably struggle with loneliness more than others. But I am also telling you that you are not a victim. Just because you've had a messed up past, doesn't mean that you have to live messed up for the rest of your life. There are things that you can do.

> Just because you've had a messed up past, doesn't mean that you have to live messed up for the rest of your life.

If you translate that to adult kids—like we men—that means we need to find connections too. In other words, we all need at least one person in our lives that we can really connect to on a heart-to-heart, soul-to-soul level. While hanging with the guys is good and we might have some close and trusted friends we would cut off our right arms for if necessary, the relationship I am talking about here will only be found with the one person you are willing to pledge your life to with the phrase: "I take you to be my wife, to have and to hold, for better or for worse, for richer, for poorer, in sickness and in health, to love and to cherish; from this day forward until death do us part."

It's no wonder when people say, "You can't live with 'em, and you can't live without 'em," that everyone nods in agreement.

Key #2
It Is Not Good for Man to Be Alone

~

And the LORD God said, It is not good that
the man should be alone; I will make him
an help meet for him
Genesis 2:18

~

Somehow God built a vacuum into us that can only be filled by connecting with other people—and specifically for men, to women. Without that connection physically, emotionally, spiritually, and mentally, we can simply turn into a mess.

No wonder, despite the greatest health care in the world and the greatest times of material prosperity in history, people are still so sick today. Loneliness is an epidemic that no one seems to know how best to treat.

ARE WE BEING ENTERTAINED TO DEATH?

We live in the information age; we're spending more and more time with PCs, TVs, cell phones, text messengers, PDAs, and plugged into iPods, so that we're missing out on the life going on around us. We may be right in the midst of a busload of people, a gym full of sweaty bodies, or in a city full of millions of people, but we are more isolated than ever before. I was walking down the street the other day and saw six young people walking together, all talking to someone else on their cell phones! Whatever happened to talking with the people you are actually with? It's almost like we are more comfortable with disembodied voices.

> The pain of loneliness can be so great that people will wish they could die rather than continue to face it.

All of these things are creating even more isolation and loneliness in our lives. And there's something about loneliness that will literally steal your hope for the future. The pain of loneliness can be so great that people will wish they could die rather than continue to face it.

When we are lonely, we feel empty inside and we can't figure out why. We all have an empty spot inside of us that can only be filled by connecting to others and connecting to Jesus.

What we sometimes do is try to fill that emptiness with drugs. We try to fill it with booze. We try to fill it with ungodly relationships. We try to fill it by buying all of the latest electronic toys, the biggest TVs, the nicest boats, the coolest motorcycles. We try to fill it by stuffing our bank accounts with money. But none of these satisfy. In fact, all they do is deepen the loneliness. A great majority of people who flip out and lose control are people who have grown up isolated.

If you are doing drugs, the drugs are the fruit of an emptiness inside you. If you are an alcoholic, it's the fruit that's being manifested in your life. It says in some way you are not filling that emptiness. None of these things will do any more than take the edge off of that hollow throbbing in our hearts. I tell you, there is no greater long-term pain than the ache of loneliness.

And guess what? Just getting married doesn't solve the problem either. As the Russian writer Anton Pavlovich Chekhov said, "If you fear loneliness, then don't get married." Leave it to a Russian to figure out the depths of cold possible between a man and wife each clinging to their sides of the bed in the middle of a Siberian winter. There is nothing worse than when it's colder in that bed than it is outside. Loneliness has indeed become the great American disease, but thank God there is a cure.

SURVIVOR SKILLS

If we are going to keep from being lonely in this life, there are some things we are going to have to do—there are some changes in our lives we are going to have to make. When you see that you are lonely because you are alone, you've got to stop and make some decisions to change the way you are living. After all, one of the definitions of insanity is continuing to do the same thing expecting different results. If what we have been doing has gotten us somewhere we don't want to be, then it is time to back up and take another road!

Often, we want to blame somebody else or some circumstance for our loneliness. We want to say we're lonely because we're single, or we're lonely because of who we're married to. But let me tell you, loneliness comes because you are disconnected.

The solution isn't to find who is at fault. The solution is to develop better connection skills. In order to do that, there is some groundwork we will have to lay first.

~

The formula for a happy marriage? It's the same as the one for living in California: when you find a fault, don't dwell on it.
Jay Trachman

~

A lot of the great American disconnect that is happening today is because of the break up of the family that is the result of the break-up of marriages. And why are marriages breaking up? Because after that happy, euphoric state of "being in love" wears off, we suddenly realize that we don't understand each other. We can't agree on the smallest things anymore. And where "love" before anesthetized us to each others shortcomings, now monotony has worked those same "cute little personality quirks" like sand in our gears. After you've been married for a while, every weakness gets magnified. Go long enough without dealing with these things and everything grinds to a halt.

The first step is that we need to deal with the unre- solved issues and baggage in our own lives before we can really connect with another person.

ME FIRST!

You see God knew what kids were capable of, and that every kid needed to be double-teamed until they knew how to play defense for themselves. And if possible, others in the community—den mothers, baseball coaches, neighbors, youth leaders, and the like—could substitute in from time to time to give the parents a breather, but in the home, every kid would be double- teamed. In fact, one study states that every kid should have five adults other than their parents that they can go to if they have a problem. That's a far cry from the single- parent world we live in today.

There is a method to the madness of life: we are born as babies so that we can grow into the world. We are born smaller and weaker than adults so that they can handle us and overpower us if needed for our own good (and even then we still need to be double-teamed!). Parents are built-in life coaches who have been over all the same territory themselves that we experience as we grow from childhood through adolescence into adulthood. Developmentally, children are very selfish because the first thing they need to figure out in the world is who they are and how that relates to their world. It is a quandary that continues through adolescence as we try to synchronize what we have learned about ourselves, and the needs of the world around us. The thought was that by adulthood we would have mastered our "selfish" world enough to balance it with the needs of those around us, and we could contribute to our world as we were destined to do.

Why are people single? Some people are single because they haven't found anybody "good enough" for them yet. Some are single because they're so needy they push people away. Some people are single because they are sick and tired of all the relationship messes around them in their friends and families.

We need to remember that singleness is not the issue. The issue is loneliness. Many lonely people let that loneliness on the inside of them drive them to do the opposite of what they know to be good and true. If you're married and lonely, then you're more susceptible to adultery than you should be. If you are lonely, you are more susceptible to wandering the internet looking at things you know you shouldn't look at and chatting with people you know you shouldn't chat with.

No Man Is an Island . . .
But It's Still Good to Know How to Live on One!

~

Mortify therefore your members which are
upon the earth; fornication, uncleanness,
inordinate affection, evil concupiscence,
and covetousness, which is idolatry.
And have put on the new man,
which is renewed in knowledge
after the image of him that created him.
Colossians 3:5,10

~

If you are single, use it as the opportunity to work in your church or your community and seek your purpose and passion in life. Being single doesn't have to mean being lonely and talking to volleyballs. When my wife was single, she worked in her church. She said, "I'm tired of all the mess around me. I'm going to use my life as a single woman to help others." Being single is a good opportunity to get your priorities in order before you mix them in with someone else's. Too many think they will solve their problems by hooking up with someone else, but all they really do is add two new sets of problems to their life. Now they have their own problems, plus their partner's problems, and now the relationship's problems. It gives a whole new meaning to *Yours, Mine, and Ours.*

However, if you are already married and you have all of this going on, while it is more complicated, it is not impossible. Take the time to work on yourself and your relationship. Marriage does have its advantages because you are not alone—but first you will probably have to deal with some of the pain between you and your spouse in order to break down a few walls so that you don't feel so lonely anymore.

A NEW CULTURE OF SELF-INDULGENCE

One of the problems in our culture today is that we have a lot of twenty, thirty, and forty-something's—single and married—who still haven't figured out who they are and why they are here on the earth. They are twenty-seven, thirty-three, and forty-five, and still as selfish as they were when they were seven. But now they are packing and running wild on the streets. They have everything they need to reproduce and start families, but instead they are out experimenting with this equipment like a five-year-old with a box of crayons. No one has taught them that with ability comes responsibility. They seem to want to live a life of fun and games right up until retirement with no responsibility to anyone but themselves, and as a result, our culture and families are suffering.

> People don't have mid-life crises any more; they have one every four or five years because they don't know who they are even into their fifties!

Today we have twenty-five year olds exiting college still relying on their parents to do everything for them—

and are upset with their bosses for actually expecting them to do something on the job. All kinds of studies today say that this generation will change careers more times than any before it—no wonder! People don't have mid-life crises any more; they have one every four or five years because they still won't know who they are even into their fifties!

Key #3
You Can Never Be Your Woman's Man Until You Are Your Own Man

I actually heard a story the other day about a college freshman, when having a dispute with a counselor over her schedule, pulled out her cell phone, called her mom and handed the phone to the counselor saying something like, "Here, you work this out with her."

If our kids don't have the skills to deal with the small interactions of life by the time they leave home, how can we expect them to understand what it takes to commit to the life-long relationship that marriage is supposed to be?

The problem is that they don't know who they are and what their purpose in life is, so how are they supposed to relate with someone else who has no idea who they are or what their purpose is about either?

The mistake we seem to be making is that marriage is not about joining our bodies together—that's the easy part—but it is a covenant with God, it's about joining our hearts and destinies together. It is not just a union to give birth to children, but also one to give birth to dreams, aspirations, and purpose. As Ernesto Cortez, Jr., put it in an article entitled, "The Broader Context of Community": "It has been said that it takes a village to raise a child. Well, do we know what it means to build a village?"

~

When we are motivated by goals that have deep meaning, by dreams that need completion, by pure love that needs expressing, then we truly live life.
Greg Anderson

~

Until you know where you are going in life, what you want to accomplish, and have a platform firm enough to build that life upon, you have no firm place to stand from which you can really love another person.

And love, my friend, is much, much more than that dopey feeling you get when you look at a women who has it all working together to get your attention.

WHAT IS YOUR "SPECIAL PURPOSE"?

Have you ever seen Steve Martin in the movie, *"The Jerk"*? Steve plays the character Navin Johnson. Navin leaves home and joins the circus and is waylaid by an Amazon of a woman who takes him to her trailer to teach him what his "special purpose" is. After a few months, Navin falls for another girl and discovers that there is much more to life and his "special purpose" than he had been learning.

That is a pretty good illustration of the way things are in the world today. From E! Entertainment news to Hollywood to MTV reality shows, you would think that our "special purpose" in life was about hooking up, but just as Navin learned, pleasure is not a purpose and that true fulfillment is a byproduct of God's perfect purpose for our lives.

No, the purpose of being single is not to test out your prowess with as many different women as possible and party every night until you can't find your way home. Such things will not fill that hole inside of you, but only numb it until one day you wake up and realize you have never gotten what you were really after and have utterly wasted your life. Nor is it a stage of life to rush through trying to find a spouse as soon as possible, rushing from relationship to relationship thinking that finding a woman—any woman!—is what will meet your needs. You can't fill loneliness with sex, drugs, extreme sports, bungee jumping, or even marriage—all you will do is magnify it later on down the road somewhere. Sex without true friendship will never fulfill. True friendship comes from joining purposes and hearts, not joining bodies! Instead try filling that emptiness inside of you with purpose and service to your world, and then when you find a woman who has the same dreams and direction in life, you can join up to tackle the world together.

COMPLETE OR COMPETE?

As I said before, you will never really be your woman's man until you are your own man. And I will tell you the truth; we have a real shortage of real men—of husbands, fathers, and mentors--in our world today.

You see, marriage is made to complete the two people who come into it. Now that does not mean single people are half-people, but that there is a synergy when two people who have it together come together to become one. If they don't have it together on their own first, then they don't complete one another, they compete for one another's attention—and what should be a place of harmony and cooperation becomes a war zone. Instead of working together, they are working against each other, and how can two people work together if they don't even know what they are working for? Where there is no purpose, people have no hope, and where there is no hope, people have no self-control. They will destroy each other through selfishness trying to get what they want with little thought for the other. Believe me. I've been there, done that, and gotten the t-shirt. That is not what living is all about.

> You see, marriages are made to complete the two people who come into them.

No Man Is an Island . . .
But It's Still Good to Know How to Live on One!

WAKE UP AND SMELL THE COFFEE

No matter where you are in life, it is not too late to try to fix this. You can start right where you are—in fact, that is really the only place you can start. Maybe you are young and single with your whole life before you and this is exactly the right message for you at the right time, or perhaps you have already blown up two marriages and are wondering what you are going to do now, or perhaps all is going well with your spouse and you would like it to stay that way, or perhaps you are in the middle of blowing up your marriage and want to figure out how to keep it from crashing and burning. I'm telling you, you have to start by pursuing your true purpose in life, and when you find that, become the man who has what it takes to fulfill it. Then from there, you have a place to reach out to your wife or a woman you may be dating and do what is best for her because you know what is best for you. You then have a place to give from rather than coming to her in need looking for as much as you can get.

Of course, don't let me gloss things over and make it sound like finding your purpose is an easy thing to do, because it isn't. I don't have a great amount of space to go into it here, and there are some great books out there on finding purpose, but short of all that, finding your life's purpose isn't that hard either. You just need to start moving out in search of it and let your heart start leading the way. Finding your purpose will not happen if you are sitting on the couch.

Your purpose in life is always attached to your God given talent, likes and dislikes, as well as your natural talents and abilities. Let's say you are good with kids and love football and math—you may be a teacher who will also be a coach—or maybe you will be an accountant who leaves work early to coach a Peewee team.

Or what if you are good at public speaking and helping people agree on things—then perhaps you were meant to work in government or politics. Maybe you love to work with your hands and make things happen, and then maybe you are called to be a contractor as I was earlier in my career. There are a number of callings for any number of occupations or hobbies in the world. What you need to do is start plugging into your likes and dislikes, gifts and talents, and see where they start to lead you. As you move towards them, you will know if they are central to your purpose or not.

Far too many people go into the workforce looking to earn a paycheck and forget that their communities need them. It is one thing to be a banker, but it is quite another to be one who does all that he can to see that the youth center across the street has everything it needs to help kids in the neighborhood. It is amazing how much one person can do—think of the Jimmy Stewart character, George Bailey, in *It's a Wonderful Life*. Here is a guy who never got to do all the things he had dreamed of, but because he was willing to always do the right thing, he changed the fate of hundreds. But there is also a big difference between that guy and one who is into building his community just for the money.

We make a mistake if we think that earning a living is all it is about because the truth is that real living comes from what we give. So you may already have a job to cover rent and food, but what are you giving back to your community? Are you volunteering somewhere? Are you a member of a local church that is doing something to make a difference for families in the area? Are you a member of an organization that builds houses for the homeless, or works to provide hurricane relief to a torn up area, or any number of other things that give back to the world you were born into? A lot of times purpose reveals itself when we serve others.

Too many people think that a paycheck is there for them to live off of, but I am telling you, what it should really be doing is freeing you to follow the dreams that are in your heart. The luckiest people are those that find a job following their purpose— they get paid to make their dreams come true! But these are also the people who know where they are going in the world and find occupations and not just get jobs. They see work as doing what they love; not just a way to pay for their new big screen TVs or tricked out cars.

> A lot of times purpose reveals itself when we serve others.

Single people have more freedom to explore these things than married people do, because single people don't have the same responsibilities to make sure that their family is covered at the end of each month and the mortgage on their five-bedroom house is paid. Single people can still live to find their dreams, married people should be living to support each other's dreams.

Singles, take advantage of your singleness. When you are single, you can work night and day if you want to and don't have to answer to anyone as to when you've got to be home. So while you're single, take advantage of your singleness. Volunteer in your community and your church because if you've got the right attitude you can do a whole lot more while you are single than you can when you're married. Leave the partiers to waste their lives and start living yours now, don't put it off until you are too busy raising a family.

One final thing to think about is that your purpose may not always stay the same. Sometimes for half of your life you work to save up money so that you can retire early and then give back to your community or do aid work in another part of the world. For me, I spent much of my life in construction, but now, as a pastor, I write and speak all over the world and help others live the best lives they can, and I have to admit that my wife and I have never been happier as we both pursue what our hearts tell us we should be doing.

READY TO LAUNCH?

Just as finding your purpose takes work, so does keeping your marriage relationship going great. It is one thing to find your place in the world and finally decide you want to share it all with someone special, but it is another to do it, and quite another to keep it going well. It is also important to understand who we are in relationship to each other and what your roles are in building a family together. So read on, I think you will find some things that really surprise you!

Chapter Three

DATING, MARRIAGE, AND LOVE

The meeting of two personalities is like the contact of two chemical substances: if there is any reaction, both are transformed.

Carl Jung

Ah . . . the dating game.

So, if we can't stand the thought of being alone in life (and if you can, there is certainly nothing wrong with that; some people live very happy lives single) and don't want to be lonely in marriage, then it is good to learn the art of the dating.

Guys, if you really want companionship, love, and a lasting relationship in life with the woman of your dreams, you have to change some things. Relationships take work, and dating is for practicing healthy relationships starting with friendship, and then seeing what develops—or doesn't—beyond that. Get that down and the intimacy will be all the better when it is time.

"THERE'S CHEMISTRY BETWEEN US"

From about thirteen on, when adolescence hits, our bodies are gearing up to procreate. It is funny that during the same time our reproductive organs go from childhood to adulthood in just a few months, our brains experience the greatest chaos and change of our lives. Though our brains have grown about as big as they ever will by the age of fifteen or so, they begin an intense rewiring when the hormones kick in to start puberty, and this process doesn't stop until about the age of twenty-four for women and as late as twenty-eight or twenty-nine for men. When I heard that I suddenly understood how some of the guys I went to school with and did stupid things with went on in their thirties and forties to run large corporations, businesses, and nonprofits. Men, we do get better with age!

> Men, we do get better with age!

I don't want to get too technical, but the way it works is that we basically have four parts to our brain that mature in a specific order as we grow through adolescence into adulthood. The first is the part that controls physical coordination—thus preadolescence is that time most of us fell in love with playing sports. The second is the motivational/risk-taking brain—the part that makes us excited to do the crazy things we love and want to dare to do things we haven't before. The third part is the emotional brain, the part of us that puts passion and fear into our lives. And last but not least is our analytical brain—

the part that can balance out all of the options and determine which is the wisest and which is the most foolish.

Now, all of these develop before we are in our teens, but there is major rewiring going on between fifteen and twenty-something. The mind is changing—developing things that get used and storing things from childhood we don't need access to anymore. It is sort of a use it or lose it situation, which is why we tend to remember high school pretty clearly, but only scraps and pieces before age ten. While all of this is happening, our function in adolescents and early twenties tends to emphasize the use of these parts of the brain in order of their development. We get the physical coordination part right, are motivated to do what is pleasurable and what we are good at, feel the emotion connected to those successes, and then eventually figure out whether those things were good or bad, wise or foolish, considerate of others or selfish.

Movies provide one of the best examples of this. Teens and adults tend to like different films for just these reasons. I remember, for example, when I took one of my sons to see the movie *Speed* (disclaimer: if you haven't seen it by now I am going to spoil it for you here). He thought it was so great. What an action flick! He was ecstatic as we drove home in the car about what a great movie it was. Finally, after about ten minutes of bouncing in his seat raving about it, he asked me how I liked it. I said I thought it was kind of dumb. He was shocked. "Why?" he wanted to know. "It didn't make sense," I told him. "The bad guy figures out that the people on the bus have been rescued, that the police are onto him, but he still goes to pick up the ransom money? What's with that?" He was quiet for a moment, and then said, "You're right! There he was, supposed to be so smart, and then he gets caught because he walks into a trap he even knows about. That's dumb!" Finally, the movie had reached his thinking brain and when it did, it changed everything.

This is also why some people believe that emotional intelligence is as much as twenty-five times more important than regular IQ smarts. In the book, *Emotional Intelligence* by Daniel Goleman, the story of the "marsh-mallow experiment" is told. Researchers took four-year-olds into a room from which others watched from behind a double mirror. They were told something along the line of: "I have to step out for a few minutes, but here are two marshmallows. If you would like, you can eat them before I get back, but if you wait, I will give you five marshmallows once I return." Then the researcher left. What they found was that some of the kids had the ability to delay their gratification until the researcher returned and others did not.

When tested years later, those that showed more self-control and waited, ended up more successful overall in their lives regardless of how smart any of them were. Their "EQ"—ability to control their emotions long enough and delay meeting their immediate desire because of a better reward down the road—was more important than their IQ. Why? Because they showed the same ability that others demonstrate when they do their homework before they play, practice the piano before they watch TV, eat their dinner before having their dessert, wait to have sex until after they are married, and so on and so on. It is one thing to know the right thing to do, it is quite another to have the self-control and strength of will to always do it.

That is why we need to think before we date, not after, because it is only through thinking that relationships are truly built.

Let me take this to another level. When we see a woman, what is the process of "liking" her? We see her body, "She's hot!", and then, if we are still up for dating her after that—which oftentimes is the point a lot of us want to run away—then we start to talk and get to know her to discover if she has a brain or not, or if she is emotionally compatible. That is completely backwards.

Yet our wiring doesn't help us much in this either. When we "fall in love" it is as if all reason shuts down in a cloud of infatuation. It might be more accurate to call it being "love drunk." In the same way that inhibitions and judgment fall away with alcohol, when a person falls in love all the other person's flaws seem to disappear and their strengths become overpowering. In his book, *The Road Less Traveled*, Dr. M. Scott Peck describes this as

> ...a genetically determined instinctual compo-
> nent of mating behavior. In other words, the tempo-
> rary collapse of ego boundaries that constitutes
> falling in love is a stereotypic response of human
> beings to a configuration of internal sexual drives
> and external sexual stimuli, which serves to increase
> the probability of sexual pairing and bonding so as to
> enhance the survival of the species.[1]

---

[1]. M. Scott Peck, The Road Less Traveled (New York: Simon & Schuster, 1978), 89-90.

Thus the saying "Love is blind" because it seems impossible to reason with a person "in love." This euphoria is something that tends to last no more than two years, but unfortunately that still gives us plenty of time to date and get married before we ever had a chance to "sober up."

~

*Love may be blind, but marriage
is a real eye opener!*
Anonymous

~

Now this is disorienting enough, but if you have sex with a woman, there is actually an "attachment" chemical released in our brains that hooks us to that particular person. It is the same hormone that is released when a woman breastfeeds her child so that she will be attached to that child and nurture it into adulthood. Ever notice how second children never get the attention the first one does? It is because that drug decreases after use. So what happens when you have sex with several people before you are married? That hormonal, emotional glue loses its stickiness, and instead of strengthening the bonding process, you instead practice separating and tearing away from others. Then we get to marriage and can't figure out why things don't stick like they should or they did for the generations before us who emphasized waiting until marriage to have sex.

"THIS IS YOUR MIND ON DRUGS"

Remember that old commercial with the egg and the frying pan? They showed the egg and said, "This is your brain," then they cracked it into a blisteringly-hot frying pan and said, "This is your brain on drugs. Get it?"

Well that is what we do with our hearts when we sleep around. We sear them until they are calloused, hard, and burnt. What was once open and inviting is now seared and hardened. It is filled with "baggage"—hurts, past failures, fears, and mistrust. We hide it all in the closets when we date, but when we are married we pull it all out and bring it on the honeymoon with us.

As I said before, it is better to travel light into your honeymoon.

~

All marriages are happy. It's the living together
afterward that causes all the trouble.
Raymond Hull

~

Face it, sex makes you dopey. We are loaded enough with hormones when we see an attractive woman, but throw the "attachment" chemicals of sex into that and you become absolutely stupid. Have you ever had a friend "fall in love" with the wrong woman and then tried to convince him of it? He is thinking with anything but his reasonable mind! And if she is the first woman he has had sex with? He is gone, man. Burnt toast. His only hope is for something to happen and they break up sooner rather than later. Better a broken engagement than a broken marriage, especially if there are children involved who will now take the baggage of divorce into adolescence before they even date!

That is one main way we differ from animals. Animals are completely controlled by these lower parts of the brain because they have no thinking/reasonable brain, but we do. However, if we don't use it, then we are no better than they are. Thus the expression, "Men are animals!"

> My message to you is that it isn't too late to start doing it the right way.

Now you may be reading this and recognizing all of this is true because you have experienced it yourself. Been there, done that, got the t-shirt. My one comment for you is: how do you think I learned all of this?

If I had a chance, there are a lot of things I would undo in my previous relationships, but I can't. All I can do is do the best I can right now with what I have learned and share it with others hoping they don't make the same mistakes. My message to you is that it isn't too late to start doing it the right way. Sure, it will be harder for you than someone who hasn't been through all of this, but you also now know the value of doing it right. Read on. The best part of all of this is still ahead.

MARS ORBITING VENUS

There is a flipside to this coin of the way we think and feel, and it is a pretty good one. It is that if we can train ourselves to act and think in the opposite way to most of the rest of the guys around us, suddenly we will start sticking out and getting noticed for it. You will start to be like an eagle among prairie chickens. When the word gets out, you won't have trouble getting dates. Suddenly your reputation will start to work for you rather than against you.

In the dating process, you shouldn't be trying to "see how far you can get" with a woman, but see if you can become friends before anything else. Really, the whole point of dating is making friends and having fun with a member of the opposite sex. In a lot of ways, it is a field study of a Martian circling Venus trying to see if her planet is safe for him or not. If he goes into her environment, can he breathe her air? Can he eat her food? Can he communicate with her? Will she attack him? Is she friendly? They are not setting up formal treaty negotiations yet, they are just making first contact. If it fails, chalk it up as a learning experience; if it appears they are making a successful connection, and then they can see if a closer alliance is possible.

~

Dating as you know it is simply one of the most inefficient, nonproductive, haphazard and hit-and-miss ways to try and achieve one of the most important objectives of your life. It's time to do something different.
Dr. Phil McGraw

~

We need to realize that all dating should not necessarily be aimed at finding a mate. A lot of it, especially before you are twenty or so, should be for getting to know the opposite sex and learning how to talk and relate with them. Remember, until hormones got the better of us, we never wanted to have anything to do with girls. So early dating should be about friends going out to learn how the other species acts and reacts to similar things. There should be a lot of talking going on, and a lot of wondering out loud.

And guys, especially you younger ones, get this: on a date, the best way to impress a girl is to find out about her. What are her dreams for the future? What does she like to do with her time? Ask "why?" a lot and then practice what most married men have never learned to do: *active listening.* Don't sit there trying to see down her blouse or think about what you are going to say next to really charm her; sincerely listen to what she is saying and learn about the Venusians from one of them in the flesh.

Then as you get older and want to start dating girls to think about finding a mate, consider it more like courting. Sure, you can still go on fun dates, but getting more serious doesn't mean getting her into a hot tub with no one else around, it means finding out more about what is in her heart. Find out how she handles stress, disagreements, money, spending time with your family and things like that. Does she like hanging out with your friends or does she fight with them all the time? Is she honest with you? It's not a bad thing to approach courting someone as you would go into a business partnership, because if you get married, that's what a marriage contract is, the highest form of partnership legally possible between two entities.

When eagles begin to court, the female carries a stick into the air and flies around looking for a prospective suitor. When one comes, she flies up to a certain height and drops the stick. If he dives and catches it, it was a successful first date! Then she goes and gets a bigger one, drops it, and the courting continues this way. If he drops the stick, the courtship is over. He is not capable enough to provide for her and their young. But if he keeps catching it, she'll go get a bigger stick, fly a little bit lower, and drop it again. He's got to keep catching the sticks until she is sure he can handle anything the world with throw at him. If he can't cut it, she will kick him to the curb and go find a better prospect.

Seems like we should be at least as smart as birds, don't you think?

THE MATE TEST

The reason people get hurt in relationships is mainly because of two reasons: 1) they don't know who they are and where they are going, so they compromise to try to fill this void with a relationship, or 2) they put meeting their own needs and desires in front of what is best for the other person.

The proper match in a relationship headed for marriage is some strange math. It goes something like this: 1 + 1 = 1. In other words, one whole person connects with another whole person, and together they become unified into one heart and mind. To do this though, a person needs both a healthy sense of self that acts as a base from which that person can reach out and love others. It is the balance of the old saying, "Love your neighbor as yourself." Until you are secure in yourself, how can you ever trust anyone else?

Thus the mate test has two sides: not only 1) is this the woman I want to spend the rest of my life with and with whom I can trust my heart, but also 2) am I the type of person someone would want to spend her life with and who can be trusted with her heart? So as you look at each of the categories below, think of both of these: 1) how do I find the ideal woman that meets them for me, and 2) how do I meet them for the woman of my dreams.

∽

No man is free who is not master of himself.
Epictetus

∽

Dating can be a pretty artificial relationship that is based mostly on "making the sale." It is a lot like hunting. We put on the right clothes and even the right smells so that we look like a friend instead of a predator. We always have our best foot forward and too often our eye on the prize. This is a tough cycle to break. The key is to get behind the artificiality of dating and try to see what the person is like the rest of the time. Pay attention to the little quirks you think are so cute now, because they will probably be the little things that drive you crazy later. And realize your brain is hormoned up and is glossing over some important issues—its reason center is cloudy enough on its own, but when you start fraternizing with the opposite sex, it is gearing up for action. You have to be aware that you can't always trust your feelings, but you have to balance them with wisdom. As the old saying goes, "Love is blind," so it is good to have someone else act as the guide. Think it through. Get wisdom from others. Your body is made so that it will function pretty well with anyone of the opposite sex, but your heart—and even your bank account—are not.

Key #4
Don't Make Major Decisions about Marriage While "Under the Influence" (Of Love That Is) Balance It by Looking at Her Whole Person

When you're interested and feeling attracted to someone, the tendency is that you'll overlook stuff. "Oh, I know she's got a bad temper, but she doesn't do it to me, so no biggy." "Oh, I know she does drugs, but after we get together she said she'd stop." "I know she sleeps around, but if we get married she'll be a one-man woman." If she is cranky before you marry her, she will stay cranky afterwards. If she is chronically unhappy before you marry her, you are nuts if you think that is going to change just because she now has you. If she has different ideas about life, the universe, and everything than you do before you are married, what makes you think that will change after you are married? I'll tell you, crazy goes clear to the bone!

Here are some things to think about as you get beyond casual dating into looking for the right person to spend the rest of your life with:

1. How do they treat other people?

It is easy to put on a good face when you are meeting someone for the first time. It is easy to be nice because we all want to be liked. However, as we get to know someone more, we tend to relax our "best foot forward" posture and get more real.

When you are getting to know someone you are interested is spending your life with, look at how she treats the people she knows the best. How does she talk about her longtime friends when they aren't around? How does she treat them when they are? How does she speak about her family? Now granted, dysfunctional families are everywhere these days, but if she goes on and on about them when you are dating, will that stop after you are married? No way. Plus, when she is with her friends, what will she be saying about you? If they are not faithful to their friends, what makes you think they will be faithful to you?

How does she talk about other authority figures in her life? If she is a rebel now, she isn't going to magically transform after marriage. If she has no respect for others now, do you really think she will respect you when you start making decisions around the house that she doesn't like?

Now don't misunderstand. I think wives and husbands should make as many decisions together as they can, but what happens when there is a disagreement? Every husband is treated a little like the way the wife treated her father—he is usually the man she had the most practice relating to as she grew up. If she is never civil to him, chances are when you have a disagreement with her she will treat you pretty much the same way. When the chips are down, is that something you can calmly deal with or not?

> If she is a rebel now, she isn't going to magically transform after marriage.

Is she honest with her close friends or does she lie to them regularly? Does she keep her promises? Does she speak truthfully in a tactful way so that others can benefit from her thoughts, or does she just tell people whatever they want to hear? Is she a gossip? Does she play games with people? Is she manipulative to get what she wants from them? Does she use guilt trips on people to get them to do what she wants? Does she obsess about little things? Is she really someone you want to have as your best friend for the rest of your life?

2. How does she handle money?

Now I know that must sound pretty superficial to be the number-two question, but the truth of the matter is if you want to understand a person's heart, one of the best ways is to see how they handle their pocketbook. Remember what I said about emotional intelligence and delayed gratification? Well, in real life it is not marshmallows but money we do that with. Emotionally intelligent people will master their money rather than becoming slaves to credit card companies. They will work and save before they spend, not buy everything they want on credit. What does her credit report look like?

Did you know that because most people don't pay off their credit cards every month that the average cost of something purchased with a credit card is 112 percent higher then what it was originally? Do you really want to marry someone who is willing to spend twice as much on everything because she can't wait to save and buy it with cash?

~

A woman is like your shadow—follow her, she flies;
fly from her, she follows.
Chamfort

~

Another thing is what does she spend her money on? Think about that for a moment in your own life. What do you spend money on? We spend money on what we love. When someone comes over to your house do they see bookcases full of books, or the latest, biggest HDTV? Do you have a DVD collection of your favorite movies or your favorite porn? Do you have the nicest car or a solid retirement plan already growing? Do you work hard to pay your bills or are you trying to find someone else to pay them? Do you give to charities or impulsively buy things you want and then rent a storage unit to keep them in? How selfish or how giving you are will show up with what you do with your time and money; as will how much you are planning for the future versus how much you are swept up by what you want today.

Now there is nothing wrong with having nice things, but how you get them makes all the difference in the world. If the person you are dating is not willing to put away for tomorrow before they spend today, then they may likely be someone who mortgages your future together just so that she can have what she wants today. After all, married couples fight about money more than almost anything else; and financial problems are commonly sited as leading causes for divorce.

3. How is her general attitude towards life?

Negative people with no sense of humor or ability to keep things in perspective can be very hard to live with. Does she always have an issue with someone? Can she forgive easily? Is she always suspicious of others or does she get jealous easily? Is she a constant flirt with others around you? Is she charming at one point and then manipulative at another? Does she dwell on problems for days at a time or find ways to pull herself out of them? Does she have the proper balance between having fun and being serious? Does she party too hard and seem to avoid the issues of life, or does she engage with others to make a difference where she can and not obsess over the things she can't?

4. Do you have compatible world views and faith?

Different faith backgrounds can be more difficult to transcend in a relationship than different cultural backgrounds. Where do you find truth in the universe, or do you just think everything is relative? If one of you believes that Christianity and the Bible are reasonable sources of purpose and meaning for your life and the other is Buddhist, unless you both become rather milk toast about your views, you are in for some pretty serious disagreements down the road. Not only that, but you will cut yourself off from communities that can help you when things get rough. The thought that "It takes a village to raise a child," is a little off. It takes a family to raise a child, but a village to keep a family together. Today in our larger communities, the closest most of us will get to living in a village or small town where every-one knows and supports us is in a community of faith such as a church or synagogue. If one spouse is going to one and the other to another, where is the village that keeps your family whole? What are the principles that you will gather around to keep your marriage strong?

And avoid "missionary" dating where you think you will convert the other person to your religion or way of thinking before or soon after you marry.

5. Is she a helper or a dictator?

One of the best ways to determine if a person is both humble and hopeful enough to make a relationship work is if they are willing to give of themselves to others, or a cause they believe in. This could be money, but when you are younger, it more generally means time. A nonprofit organization such as a youth program, aid organization, or faith-based community service group is a much better place to find a spouse than at a singles' bar or a party. This shows that the person is willing to lend a helping hand to make a difference rather than just looking to "have a good time" and please themselves. If they are willing to work hard just to help others for nothing in return other than the satisfaction of helping others, then chances are, that person will be a better spouse to work together with you to build a family (being a mom or dad rarely pays well in short-term dividends!).

~

A man falls in love through his eyes, a woman through her ears.
Woodrow Wyatt

~

Also, find out how she works with others. Does she always automatically take the place of the boss, or can she follow along as easily as she can lead? Does she expect people to do things she wouldn't be willing to do herself? Does she lead through example or through nagging? Can she work and get her hands dirty for what she believes in, or is she too wrapped up in her self to really care about others?

Most people are looking for talent, and they're looking for beauty. They're looking on the outside for a mate, when the most important matters are on the inside. Those that rise above the crowd—who show they have what it takes to make a solid relationship on the inside—are usually those with hearts sincere in wanting to help others.

FIRST THINGS FIRST

If you can't find someone who will be your friend and put her shoulder to the wheel with you to make a life together, then it doesn't matter how things are in the bedroom. I have never known hot sex to stay hot or keep a relationship or marriage together, but I do know becoming better friends and sharing purpose in life can make sex better between couples. Believe me, it doesn't take an incredible amount of compatibility to procreate—all you have to do is look around you for evidence of that. But it does to make a marriage last a lifetime.

~

A tree is known by its fruit; a man by his deeds. A good deed is never lost; he who sows courtesy reaps friendship, and he who plants kindness gathers love.
Saint Basil the Great

~

The problem is that being single or lonely can make us feel desperate. It makes us willing to lower our standards to get what we think we need. I am telling you though, if you are willing to compromise to get something that will only partially fulfill you, then all you will ever be is partially fulfilled. If you have the attitude, "Well, at least it is better than nothing," I can almost guarantee you will be wrong. The pain of a broken relationship that has gone too deep too fast and sets off all those hormones and attachment chemicals in our brains will hurt us far worse than developing the self-control needed to wait for the right one. If you are not finding the right kind of person out there, then work on yourself to become the right person to be found by the type of woman you want.

You have to rise off the ground and get up into their realm to be noticed by the other eagles. If you stay in the pits, all you will ever find are prairie chickens.

So it is a good thing to know to look for these important characteristics, but it is another thing to know how to go about discovering them. That's where the next key, communication, comes in. The reason too many marry the wrong person or can't keep the relationship going once they are married probably has more to do with communication than anything else. I'll tell you, wherever you are, it is a good time to work more on your communications skills, so let's get started.

Chapter Four

UNDER CONSTRUCTION

The meaning of life is creative love. Not love as an inner feeling, as a private sentimental emotion, but love as a dynamic power moving out into the world and doing something original.

Tom Morris,
If Aristotle Ran General Motors

I used to be a building contractor that worked on large buildings like shopping malls and apartment buildings. In all the time I did that, I never had anyone come into a structure we were in the midst of building and ask, "Hey, what's wrong with you? The bathroom's don't work—in fact, there aren't even any toilets?" or "What's wrong with the elevator? There isn't even a button for it yet?"

Why not? Because as they walked into the framed building, they knew it was still under construction and that all of those details would be added as the building was closer to being finished. At that point, they just wanted to know that we had the plumbing or electrical fixtures installed correctly depending on how close we were to being finished. Building inspectors don't wait until the whole structure is finished before they come in and see if everything is where it should be—if they did it would be possible for a shifty contractor looking to cut some corners to hide things not up to code beneath the walls. Even in the midst of the mess of construction, the inspector can tell if things are headed in the right direction and if the blueprints are being followed.

When we meet in relationships, we need to see things in a very similar way. If we are dating in our twenties, then we can't expect to find someone with the wisdom of our parents and their financial futures already in the bank. We are meeting people "under construction." We can't wait to be perfect or find the perfect person before we get married, or else the whole world would be single!

Instead of looking for the finished project, however, like a person looking for the right home, we are inspectors. We are dating people who are in the process of growing towards their potentials. While we can't expect everything to be in place and functional yet, we can check their blueprints for the future, see if their foundations are solid, check their structural integrity, and the like. We can "inspect" the progress of their construction to see if it is heading towards stability or should be condemned.

Yet too often, we get so caught up in the outward appearances and the pictures they draw of themselves, we buy what we think is the house of our dreams only to find it built on a poor foundation with faulty wiring. The house is doomed to collapse unless it catches on fire and burns to the ground first. Either way, we are in trouble.

~

Women marry men hoping they will change.
Men marry women hoping they will not.
So each is inevitably disappointed.
Albert Einstein

~

Now if you are already in such a relationship, there is still hope, because you can both work together to strengthen the foundation of your relationship or redo the wiring afterwards, it will just be more work than if you had gotten it right in the first place. Whether you are married already or single, if you pay attention to some simple guidelines, you can stabilize your relationship to be solid and safe for a lifetime.

One of the things we must realize is that although we know our partners will grow as time goes by, there is very little we can do to insure that they will grow in exactly the ways we would like. If the person is inherently selfish now, no matter how beautiful she is, it is unlikely that will change much in the years to come. If she is inflexible in arguments now, she will probably not change just because she marries you. If she flirts with every guy she meets now, being married to you probably won't change that. If she is bad with her money now, she is unlikely to be any better with your money once you've both said your vows. You can do little to make sure she changes in the way you want, however, you can make changes in yourself that will make change easier for her. Most of the time if we are willing to change ourselves, it is easier for others to follow our example.

> ## Key #5
> You Will Never Find the "Perfect" Mate
> But At Least Make Sure the Basics Are
> Compatible.
> No Matter What Happens,
> You Need to Beware
> of the "Relationship Destroyers"

As I look at relationships under construction, I see five main things that will cause a relationship to crumble. If we counteract these in our own lives, then that is a huge step towards ensuring our relationship is on a solid foundation even before any of the walls, fixtures, wiring, or anything else goes up—in other words, with the right foundation, other things are much easier to fix; with a poor foundation, oftentimes it is easier to tear the whole thing down and start from scratch.

If the right qualities and personality traits are present in the other person in satisfactory amounts, then we know we can have hope for our future together no matter what we might face. If these are not in place, then we can be sure there will be rough storms ahead, and unless we can strengthen these areas in each other, our relationship may not stand.

If you look at any index of what causes stress, you will see that most of those at the top have to do with relation-ships. Some, such as a spouse or child dying in an accident, we may not have any control over, but there are some things we can do to strengthen our relationships to avoid other kinds of break ups. If we are not careful, relationships will fall apart and leave us hurting. Your relationship will make or

> If you look at any index of what causes stress, you will see that most of those at the top have to do with relationships.

break you, so it is important to know how to keep it together as a basis for having it bring you joy rather than stress and heartache.

So here are the five main areas we need to address in order to help our relationships flourish instead of flounder.

1. SELFISHNESS

Every problem you will ever have in a relationship begins with selfishness. Selfishness unchecked destroys marriages. Selfishness is at the base of every conflict, dis-agreement, and argument you have with another person, and in long-term relationships it is a slow-working poison that will sap the joy, strength, and confidence from every-one involved. When it's all about me and what I want, it isn't too long before both people in the relationship are pulled into the vacuum that selfishness creates.

The problem is that selfishness is both cunning and relentless. It will disguise itself as affection and generosity to get what it wants. It will hide itself to fool both the person who is being selfish and the person it is trying to draw in to get what it wants. It intoxicates the person being selfish to the point that it blinds that person to the fact that others have needs as well. At the beginning of every relationship the selfish person can be charming, courteous, outgoing, and compassionate, but the reason is that this person has learned that showing their selfishness undisguised to others will not get their needs met. So it is that at the beginning of every relationship everybody seems to care more about the other person than themselves, but eventually the person's selfishness will become obvious.

In *Staying Close*, authors Dennis and Barbara Rainy talk about what it can be like during the first five years of marriage. In the first year, if your wife gets the sniffles, it's: "Baby, Darling, I'm so worried about that sniffle you have. I've called the paramedics to come and rush you to the hospital for a checkup and for a good week of rest because you worked so hard. You know you need some rest. And I know you don't like hospital food, so I've arranged for gourmet meals to be brought to you."

Then, after the second year of marriage, it's like: "Sweetheart, I don't like the sound of that cough. I've arranged for the doctor to come and make a house call. Let me tuck you in bed, Baby."

Then after the third year, it's: "You look like you've got a fever. Why don't you drive yourself to the pharmacy and get yourself some medicine, and I'll watch the kids while you're gone."

In the fourth year of marriage it goes something like this: "Now, Baby, just be sensible. After you've fed and bathed the kids, and washed the dishes, and vacuumed the carpet, you really ought to go to bed."

Then by the fifth year of marriage, it becomes: "For Pete's sake! Do you have to cough so loud? I can't hear the TV. Would you mind just going in the other room while I watch this TV program? You sound like a barking dog!"

Laugh or cry, but it is all too true. The more comfortable we are around someone, the more our selfishness comes out.

Now, we need to realize that at our core, selfishness is necessary to some degree. As children we are always selfish because it is how we as helpless infants let the world know we are hungry, need to be changed, or want to be held. When a baby is born its first words are me, me, me. Their next words are no, no, no. It's all about them demanding attention. We cry out with little regard to the time of day, what others are doing, or how our selfishness is affecting anyone else. It is our way of testing how trustworthy and safe the world is. As we learn that others around us are willing to sacrifice for us as we grow up, we learn that we can trust others, and then somewhere in our adolescence, we begin to develop the stability in ourselves to be able to give back. At this stage selfishness must turn to self-reliance to build a confidence in oneself to be a contributor rather than a taker. Selfishness will always be there, but now the focus on ourselves should switch to making ourselves better human beings rather than someone who is only focused on getting whatever we want.

However, in an age of disconnection and isolation, too many don't grow up in this kind of loving environment, so the selfishness is never tamed and put into its proper place and that is to focus on how to compensate for our own weaknesses and be a blessing to others through our strengths. So instead of learning to be a giver, we become more cunning and subtle in our selfishness so that we look like givers, but in the end are interested in nothing but satisfying our own desires.

In order to build healthy relationships, you have to be a true giver. All relationships require give and take, but if it is always take, take, take, things will begin to melt down sooner or later. If you're going to have a successful marriage, the grip of selfishness has to be broken, no matter how dysfunctional your past may have been.

However, we can never completely curb our selfishness, and so society uses it to get what it wants from us. It encourages us to be self-centered, and then uses that self-indulgence to get our consumer dollars. We are told, "If it feels good do it," even if it hurts other people. We hear slogans like, "Obey your thirst," "Have it your way," "We do it all for you." It's all about obeying any urge or desire that you may have, regardless of how it affects anyone else in the world.

~

Brigands demand your money or your life;
women require both.
Samuel Butler

~

Though it makes these advertisers and their clients big money, self-centeredness ultimately causes destruction wherever it's found. Look for example at what happened to the Philadelphia Eagles in 2004. With basically the same team that took them to Super Bowl XXXIX, they fell apart when Terrence Owens started selfishly backbiting his teammates to the point that they benched him off the season, despite the fact that he is arguably the best receiver in the league. You can never build a successful team if selfishness is involved. It will unravel any accomplishment.

> You can't attack the selfishness out of someone, you have to love it out.

So if selfishness destroys relationships, then being unselfish—or selfless—is the only way to build relationships. If you are in relationship with a selfish person, the only thing you can do is to create an environment where they feel secure enough to risk giving back. Whether you are single or married, whether you have kids or don't, your home is supposed to be a place of refuge and safety, but it never will be if you don't determine to make it so. It is important that whoever comes into your home—and especially the people who live there—find it to be a place of retreat, peace, and safety. If there's fighting in your home, you've got to make up your mind that it is going to stop today. You can't attack the selfishness out of someone; you have to love it out.

Anytime you choose to be unselfish, you open the door to building a healthier relationship. However, this won't work overnight, and if all you do is feed your partner's selfishness, you won't accomplish much either. So creating such an environment takes both willingness to sacrifice *and* willingness to set boundaries that will not let your mate take advantage of your generosity to them. This takes honest engagement and a great deal of energy that most people, quite frankly, are too selfish to expend. It is often easier to give in as you would to a spoiled child so that you don't have to deal with the inconvenience. But in the long-term, you are only going to make it harder on yourself to keep the relationship together.

Anytime you are unselfish with others, it brings out the best in them. When you're unselfish, it invites people into your life and allows people to relate to you in a different way.

The truest form of unselfishness is love—not the feeling of love, but the conscious, aggressive action of love. It is an action that reaches out to others and truly expects nothing in return. It is also the tough love that lets people experience the consequences of their own selfishness so that they can learn to break its grasp upon their lives. This kind of love gives, but there is the type of giving that builds security and confidence, and there is the type of giving that spoils the person and only builds their selfishness. There is a time to say "no" as well as "yes" when you love someone. Loving someone in this way also means being willing to sacrifice for them, but not making yourself a doormat. Finding this balance in love is key.

This is also the type of love that forgives when others hurt us again and again, and it is the type of love that never gives up on anyone. It is the love that says I am committed to you and I am going to do every healthy thing I can to make our relationship work. And your partner is responsible to offer the same kind of love to you.

That is one of the main reasons shacking up never really works. It is saying as you are going into the relationship "I am not committed enough to go through the paperwork of marriage and then divorce if it doesn't work out. I am just too selfish to make that kind of a commitment."

I have found that you will live a wasted life if you don't learn how to love in this unselfish way. Without it, you will never have rewarding relationships with anyone in your life, whether it is with your spouse, your children, coworkers, or friends. It is tough to do, but the rewards I have seen are always worth the effort.

> Key #6
> Above All Else,
> Beware of Selfishness;
> It Is at The Root of Every Relationship Problem
> You Will Ever Face

One of the ironies of selfishness is that we can never help another person to rid themselves of it until we rid ourselves of it. We must always deal with our own selfishness before that of others. Of course, selfishness even fools us, so we often need help to see it in ourselves. Because of this, I have devised a little test for you to take to see where you are selfish so that you can start there, and then start to work on keeping it from hurting your relationships.

1.   Do you put others first or yourself?

2.   Are you stingy or are you generous? Is your reputation one of being a tightwad or a cheapskate?

3.   Do you give regularly to charities or nonprofit organizations?

4.   Who is the first person you consider in making any decision?

When you look at a member of the opposite sex that you find attractive, are your first thoughts lustful? Do you see them first as a person or an object of desire?

I know some of those may sting a bit, but just consider it like an antiseptic cleaning out a wound. If you find yourself answering selfishly to any of these questions, you know where to start to keep selfishness from destroying your marriage or relationship—with taming it in your own life.

2. PRIDE

Pride is selfishness distilled into blindness to everything but your own perspective and desires. It is self-deceiving. It is what makes us feel that we are always right no matter what. Any time you have a conflict in a relationship; pride will come in and make you fight for yourself rather than for your relationship. When egos collide, sparks will fly.

Pride keeps us from hearing each other and pushes other people away. When pride comes in, we think we know it all and that if we could just get others to listen to us, then they would see we are right and agree with us. This is why we fail to listen to their perspective and we'll cut them off in the middle of sentences because we feel what they have to say doesn't matter. We

> Pride makes us unteachable and blinds us to our own faults.

become overly critical, judgmental, and stubborn. You start comparing yourself to others always thinking you are better, smarter, faster, stronger, etc., even if you aren't even close.

Pride makes us unteachable and blinds us to our own faults. We are not open to what anyone else has to say and we think we know everything we need to know to solve the problem, so it also keeps us from asking for the help we often need to really find a solution. Anytime two people have a conflict pride will keep them from reconciling. Pride makes us stubborn and then we wait for the other person to take the initiative and apologize before we step in to reconcile. It makes us overly competitive and pushes others away.

The only antidote to pride is humility, but too many mistake humility for making a doormat of themselves and so they feel it is a weakness. Humility is not always giving in, but being open to others and admitting that you don't know it all. It is being confident enough in who you are to be open to other perspectives and options. It is the ability to reach outside of yourself for answers. It's humility that holds relationships together, and helps build something stable.

The only way to live in peace is by humbling yourself enough to reach out and listen. "Honey, I hurt you and I'm sorry. If I have done something wrong, please tell me." Humility is not thinking less of yourself, but is thinking about the other person. Pride blames the other person, while humility says, "I was angry. Please forgive me." Pride is about placing blame and proving who was right; humility is about accepting responsibility for making things right no matter who was at fault.

Often the first step to healing your hurting relationship is to admit the areas you where are prideful. Once you acknowledge your pride, you can let humility work in you to be a repairer of your relationship rather than a destroyer.

3. LACK OF COMMUNICATION

Even if you have overcome selfishness and pride, if you cannot communicate well you will still have tremendous problems. One of the greatest causes of stress in relationships is poor communication. It causes misunderstandings and allows emotions to keep us from dealing with the real issues at hand. If you do not communicate properly, your relationships will fall apart.

One of the most common complaints that my wife and I hear in marriage counseling is, "My husband won't talk to me." We all know that men are not the best communicators, but we as men have to change that if we're going to build healthy relationships with our wives. Many times when relationships are falling apart, we tend to throw up our hands and want to quit. There are two tendencies in this. One is that rather than stopping to sincerely listen and understand the other person's perspective, we want to yell, name call, and assassinate their character. The second is to draw back into our caves and think the situation is hopeless because "we will never understand each other." Either way the actual issue and the feelings surrounding it are never dealt with, not because they are insurmountable, but because we can't get on the same page with our spouse to address the real issue.

~

Sigmund Freud once said, "What do women want?" The only thing I have learned in fifty-two years is that women want men to stop asking dumb questions like that.
Bill Cosby

~

The key to building relationships is to communicate in love and honesty. This is so important, in fact, that rather than going into it more here, I am going to discuss it in the next two chapters. Communication is the life blood of any relationship, so it is important to take the time to work on our communications skills if we want to keep our relationships strong.

4. INSECURITY

The fourth thing that pulls our relationships apart is insecurity. Anytime we are insecure, we tend to grow paranoid and we don't trust those around us. Then, since relationships are based on trust, we start to pull away and isolate ourselves, undermining our marriage and friendships.

The root cause of insecurity is fear. It's the fear that we won't be loved and that if others really knew us, they would push us away. So, rather than suffering that rejection, we tend to take the initiative and push them away first.

> When you see someone that is prideful and brags all the time, you can bet that they are insecure.

Anytime someone is insecure, pride will come in because we feel like the only person we can trust in the world is ourselves. When you see someone that is prideful and brags all the time, you can bet that they are insecure. This fear is the first thing that causes us to disconnect from those we love. Fear actually does three things to us in relationships. It makes us defensive, it makes us distant, and it makes us demanding.

When we're afraid of admitting our faults, we become defensive. We begin to blame others. We say, "It's not my fault, it's theirs." We try to control the other person through shame, guilt, or intimidation. They'll say things like, "What's wrong with you?", "Are you stupid?", "You'll never amount to anything", "You're no good", "I never loved you". It's all about trying to create insecurity in the other person so you can get what you want.

Insecurity prevents intimacy. It keeps you from being totally honest with the other person. It also causes you to be defensive and you start pretending that everything is okay, even when it's not. No matter who you are, you can't get close to another person if you have a fear in that relationship. I have found that the fear of rejection is one of our greatest fears. We build walls around ourselves because we don't want anyone to hurt us. We isolate ourselves and become loners as a means of protection, but all this really does is make it worse.

You are only as sick as your secrets. When you have secrets in your life, it's because you're afraid to share that part of your life with someone else, and the more secrets you have, the less intimacy and real friendship you have. It is only when you can open up to someone else about everything in your life, both your strengths and weaknesses that you will feel secure enough to trust others and only then your relationships can thrive.

5. RESENTMENT AND BITTERNESS

It's foolish to think you can hold on to any form of resentment towards someone and build a healthy relationship with them. Resentment will build a wall of bitterness in your heart that may go unnoticed if you never communicate it directly. It will eat at your insides like a cancer until you lose any ability at all to communicate without your bitterness coloring everything you say or hear. Anytime you are in a relationship, there's always the chance that you can say things that hurt those close to you and you can also be hurt by what they say to you. And because this can happen fairly regularly we need to handle it every time it happens, not letting problems fester.

If you hide hurt inside long enough it will turn into resentment and that resentment will turn into bitterness. There's something about hiding a hurt that only causes the pain to grow. Hurt may not destroy a relationship, but resentment will. They say that time heals all wounds, but the truth is that time will only make the wound deeper if we don't deal with it or try to stuff it inside instead of forgiving it. No matter who we are, we will all get hurt in relationships. But when the hurt comes, we have to learn to talk about it and get it out of our lives.

There's only one thing that will help you overcome your hurt, and that is forgiveness. We can't give in to bitterness. We can't give in to unforgiveness. We can't give in to resentment. These things will all lead to relationships falling apart.

∼

If you wish to travel far and fast, travel light.
Take off all your envies, jealousies, unforgiveness,
selfishness, and fears.
Glenn Clark

∼

Whatever you do, don't let your issues pile up on the inside of you. Don't stuff them until you explode like a volcano. You must confront your resentments so the pain can go away. Once you have talked about them, you must be willing to forgive. The only antidote to resentment and bitterness is forgiveness. Forgiveness builds relationships while resentment tears them apart. If you're going to build relationships that last, you have to release resentments and forgive. You have to learn that forgiving is better than being right, it is better than it not being your fault, and it is better than letting hurt eat you up inside to the point it becomes a real physical disease rather than an emotional one.

BUILD BRIDGES, NOT DAMS

It is the strangest thing, but true happiness only comes when you make others feel good about themselves. Because of the isolation in our society, however, people tend to burn their bridges to others and dam up the negative feelings in their hearts when they should be doing just the opposite: building new bridges and knocking down the dams.

If you can't get along with others, it's going to affect every area of your life. It's going to affect your finances. It's going to affect your work. It's going to affect how you relate with your friends and what you do in your free time. If you treat your spouse or girlfriend as though she can't do anything right, it's only a matter of time before she walks out the door.

~

People shop for a bathing suit with more care than they do a husband or wife. The rules are the same. Look for something you'll feel comfortable wearing. Allow for room to grow.
Erma Bombeck

~

Are you supporting your partner the way she needs to be supported, or are you tearing her down? Are you looking for more ways to do things together, or more ways to get away from her? Have you ever seen two people that are married, but they live two totally separate lives? They're not one flesh. They don't have any unity. Do you want to know why? Because they're selfish and self-centered. They take separate vacations, and they have separate bank accounts.

When people are selfish, they become roommates rather than helpmates. They live in the same house, they come together for sex, but they think very little of each other and do very little together. They don't have a unified purpose and undivided hopes for the future. Two visions is *division*. Before long, they will divide from each other completely.

We all seem to do better if we have the security of one person's love, one person's trust, one person's faithfulness, but when we don't support our partners properly, we open the door for trouble. Sometimes we need to remind ourselves that the point of living is giving. If we don't understand that, we'll never live a purposeful, fulfilled life, but if we do, we have a key to real joy that most of the rest of the world has no clue about. Living to love and give to your spouse will bring you more happiness and intimacy than selfishness ever will. So make the decision to start living that life today.

Chapter Five

COMMUNICATION . . . THE LIFE BLOOD OF RELATIONSHIPS

Women speak because they wish to speak, whereas a man speaks only when driven to speech by something outside himself--like, for instance, he can't find any clean socks.

Jean Kerr

Communication is a continual balancing act, juggling the conflicting needs for intimacy and independence.

Deborah Tannen
You Just Don't Understand:
Women and Men in Conversation

I magine that you live in a home that has very expensive furnishings, but a section of the roof is missing in an upstairs bedroom. One day it rains and water runs out of the room, down the stairs and onto the first floor, flooding the whole house.

So the next morning, you begin the task of cleaning everything up. You work on it for days and before you can finish, it rains again. So you wait until it is over and, somewhat discouraged, you start again. Again, just before you have everything right, it rains again, and this time it is a whopper. How long will you keep this up before you completely give up?

Of course, that is a ridiculous situation, because what you really need to do is fix the roof! However, this is exactly what we all too often do in relationships. We'd rather just keep cleaning up the mess than deal with the real cause of the problems. We'd rather take care of the symptoms than tackle curing the disease of poor communication skills in our lives. If we do this long enough, however, after a while it's easier to just move out and start over than deal with that missing section of roof, because there is nothing left in the home worth saving.

The closer someone gets to you and the more you invest in the relationship, the more conflict is possible. Anytime there is a lack of consideration, a lack of commitment, or a lack of communication, damage is done. Let it go long enough, and it can seem like there is nothing left worth trying to save.

~

A happy marriage is a long conversation which always seems too short.
Andre Maurois

~

In relationships, learning to be a good communicator is a key to everything you do. Any problem you face together and can communicate openly and effectively about, can be solved. Any issue, no matter how small, however, can derail you if you and your spouse don't communicate well. Once you are willing, there are really just a few things to remember that will help you communicate better with your friend, wife, business associate, mother, or daughter.

REVERSE THE SELECTIVE AMNESIA

Remember, men and women are different. We may not actually be from different planets, but it can sure feel like it most of the time. We see things in completely different ways, we approach issues in completely different ways, and we tend to have completely different goals in resolving the issues we face, so we shouldn't be surprised that we also communicate in completely different ways.

Men tend to take issues apart like an engine to examine each part separately trying to figure out what is wrong in a step-by-step analytical approach: women tend to take in every detail at once and react to it emotionally and intuitively. When women speak to each other, they speak volumes in just a few words. If they are speaking with another woman, that woman seems to intuitively sense what the first woman was feeling as she describes what happened. Men on the other hand just hear the facts of what happened and often don't see what the big deal is. Men wonder things like: "Why was she so offended if that is all that happened?" "How did you deduce that from so little?" "What is the logical chain of steps that got you from point A to point W?" Men want a logical, linear explanation; women seem to just *know*. While this isn't a perfect system for women, it is surprising how often it is correct when a man experiencing the exact same things wouldn't have a clue.

~

Men and women belong to different species and communication between them is still in its infancy.
Bill Cosby

~

For men, communication is really only necessary when it is needed to accomplish a goal. Without a task at hand to solve, men can go for hours without saying a word and really not even realize it or feel slighted. For women, talking is to emotional health somewhere between what breathing and eating are to physical health. When women don't talk for a while, it is like they are fasting. Every morning as we start our day, my wife has to break that fast with a good conversation that is as important to her as her morning coffee. For me, I could go into my office and not speak a word all day, solving one issue after another, and come out quite happy to plop down and relax with the paper or a book and not say a word for the rest of the evening. For men, solving tasks is the stuff of life; for women it is communication and interaction.

It's been said that women speak about 25,000 words per day, while men speak less than half of that. Men communicate because they have to. Women communicate because they can. Men communicate because it's what they have to do to make a living. For them it's a necessary evil to further their jobs or careers. When he gets home, chances are he has already met his quota of words for the day, and could be quite content to go hide in his cave and tune everything out. He is not deliberately ignoring the rest of his family; it is just that his human interaction quota has already been met until the next day. However, his wife, especially if she has been home all day working by herself with no one to talk to, is still raring to talk.

~

Do you not know that I am a woman? When I think, I must speak.
William Shakespeare

~

So, men, we have to resist the urge to tune out and listen to keep the communication lines open. Every man needs to understand a woman's need to communicate. We will lose closeness, unity, and intimacy if we don't. If we tune out, she will interpret it as our lack of caring and feel hurt. It's part of her way to get close to us. As long as she has our attention, she can be happy and feel loved.

COMMUNICATION IS MORE THAN THE EXCHANGE OF WORDS

Communication certainly is about the words you speak, but it is also much more than that. It is the tone of voice, the body language, the facial expressions, and the context of the location and the environment of where you are and who you are with.

You may notice that couples who have been together for a long time in a loving relationship start looking like each other and speaking in the same patterns. They have not lost their individuality, but have taken on a new level of communication because they understand each other more. Now a look can say as much as a whole conversation did years before. They understand each other better because they have communicated so fully in the past without shutting each other down.

So much is said without words. We need to be watching as well as listening to hear what is really being said. I have heard that over time police detectives and people in charge of interrogations can tell when people are lying by watching for certain quirks. Good poker players can figure out when others are bluffing in a similar way by studying their opponents.

~

The most important thing in communication is to hear what isn't being said.
Peter Drucker

~

In the twentieth century Carl Jung and others designed an entire method of counseling called "gestalt therapy" based on watching what a person was doing as well as what they were saying (*gestalt* is German for "whole;" the idea was they where taking in the person as a whole in what they were communicating and not just what they were saying). The thought was that the person may know something consciously that they speak out, but other unconscious issues will be communicated through their body language and tone that they may not even be aware of.

The only way to go to the next level in your relationship is to be able to communicate in a loving way that makes the other person feel safe in sharing everything with you. If you are only listening with your ears, you are likely missing some other information that could be key to understanding everything being said. If you are saying "I'm listening" with your mouth, but something else with your eyes or body language, nobody is fooled. Then there will be times that you really need to hear what is being said but because you tended to disconnect in other areas, when something important comes up, you may discover a vote of "no confidence."

> The only way to go to the next level in your relationship is to be able to communicate in a loving way...

Communication can easily break down, especially between parents and children. When parents are over eager to correct all the mistakes their kids are making, they tend to shut their kids down in conversations with them. Too often fathers can easily convince their daughters that they don't care about them because we want to shut off their rambling. I mean, you guys who are younger may think that the women you date or your wives talk too much, but you haven't heard anything until you have to give a group of thirteen-year-old girls a ride somewhere. However, dads, if you are not willing to let your thirteen-year-old ramble on when she talks with you, what will happen by the time she is sixteen or seventeen? By then, she may be facing life and death issues with friends, drugs, sex, riding with a drunk driver, or something similar, but you are the last person she would come to because you closed the communications door with her long ago.

COMMUNICATIONS SHOULD BE MIXED WITH AFFECTION

If you want to keep the lines of communication open in your relationships, you must affirm the feelings of others. You must let them know that you care, and that you are there for them no matter what. The level of communication we have with our coworkers will not work with our loved ones. In the first case, the communication lines are there for task accomplishment, but our spouses and children are much more than a list of "to dos" to be correctly checked off. They need affirmation and openness in times of uncertainty. They need to know they can share anything with us because we are on the same side in facing the problems of the world. They need to know that they can tell us something they know we don't want to hear and that we won't explode at them—not that there may not be consequences—but that they can come to us rather than being forced to go to someone else.

Face it. Accidents happen. People make mistakes. If a son or daughter, for example, went to a party, got drunk, then tried to drive home in the car and had an accident, what would happen? Do they trust you enough to know that if they got drunk at a party it would be better to call you than to try to drive home? Certainly there would be some discussion at some point about the drinking and what

Communication is a way you affirm or reject someone else.

that does, but are they avoiding calling you because the communication door is shut or because you would explode at them over the phone if they called?

Communication is a way you affirm or reject someone else. If they can't talk with you safely about casual things, how can they trust you with sensitive areas of their lives or hearts? Does your silence and body language make them think you disapprove of them? Does your tone of voice belittle them and make them feel rejected?

When you get so mad at someone you refuse to talk with them at all, there will be long-term repercussions. When you give a person the silent treatment it makes them feel a lack of support. Your silence is communicating something. Your body language is communicating something. Your attitude is communicating something. You are saying you don't love them enough to put away your own hurts and break the silence. And when it is over something little, what is going to happen when it is something big?

There are issues close to our hearts that we are all uncomfortable about talking through. They may be financial matters, they may be dreams and aspirations we have had since we were young but were belittled so much we are scared to share them, or it could even be lack of sexual satisfaction in a marriage that is making one of you contemplate adultery or divorce. If you can't communicate about it, how are you ever going to deal with it? There is a big hole in the roof upstairs that everyone is ignoring—how long will you let it ruin your home before you are willing to face it and fix it?

One easy way of showing affection when communicating is by touching. When you're talking to someone and touch their hand or shoulder, it affirms them. Even a pat on the back encourages them. It communicates love, acceptance, and that you are paying close attention to them. There's something about touching that promotes health and healing. The most well adjusted people are those who are able to communicate with touch, as well as words.

If I'm going to communicate in a better way, I need to be more affectionate. There's something about loving people that unlocks their potential—it unlocks the dreams and aspirations of their hearts and helps them see themselves as capable of realizing their dreams and aspirations. Babies who are not picked up and held can literally die from a lack of hope. Anytime we hug others, our brains release endorphins. It's the brain chemical that produces a feeling of comfort and positive energy. People who feel loved feel like they can accomplish anything; while people who don't feel loved feel like they will never amount to anything. It's been discovered that people who have pets live longer than those who don't. Married people, on average, live seven years longer than single people. We have already discussed how unhealthy loneliness is. Being positively connected to others, however, is not only healthy for our bodies, but also our worlds. We go from being people not sure of why we are alive to people high on the possibilities of life.

～

After about 20 years of marriage, I'm finally starting to scratch the surface of that one [what women want]. And I think the answer lies somewhere between conversation and chocolate.
Mel Gibson

～

If you were raised in a family that didn't do much touching, chances are that you aren't very affectionate yourself. It's hard to give away something that you never had, but if you start with your loved ones, things will begin to change. It will be uncomfortable at first, but it can make all the difference down the road for your relationships with your wife and family.

When communicating in a relationship, it's also important that you listen and not accuse. Accusations make people feel threatened, and when we are threatened communication lines are shut down completely. The common mistake many of us make in marriage is that we're so busy fixing the blame for the problem that we can't fix the problem.

There are many different ways we may try to blame our spouses. We exaggerate by saying things like, "You never. . . ." "You always . . . ." "If I've told you once, I've told you a million times. . . ." When we exaggerate, we're really just trying to place blame on the other person, but the blame game doesn't help communication. Figuring out whose fault is it is an ego trip, not an act of love on the way to resolution. All you are doing is defending your own fragile ego, not building the other person's—and worse yet, in the attempt you are tearing the other person down, not building them up.

When communicating with your spouse, don't accuse in a threatening way. Find a way to communicate your issue with love and affection so that it is heard. Once your spouse feels your affection, true healing can begin. Once your spouse feels you connecting with her in open communication, everything can progress to the next level.

If you are in a relationship today and there is very little affection, I guarantee you that it is because you feel neglected. Chances are though, that your spouse has no idea about this, but feels neglected as well. This is how too many marriages deteriorate. Both feel needs, don't communicate them, and then feel they have lost the love in their lives. Certainly feelings change, but we make a mistake when we think love is only a feeling. A lot of times, especially as a marriage progresses, love is actually a conscious decision to act affectionately towards the other person and court them all over again. When this is done, the feelings can come back stronger than ever before. That's why we must teach each other how we need to be loved. That means sitting down and talking about it and figuring out where the misunderstandings are. Reading something together like Gary Chapman's *The Five Love Languages* that discusses some of the major ways people tend to hear love could be a good place to start such a dialogue.

I have learned that love must be taught. Whether you know it or not, people are starving for affection and touching. That's why we all need to make some changes in our lives. I'm talking about hugging your kids. I'm talking about showing affection to your spouse. I believe that when a child grows up in a non-affectionate family, they tend to get involved in sex at very early ages because they feel a physical need to connect that was lacking throughout their earlier years. Anytime you see a promiscuous teenager, you can bet that they were starved for loved growing up. In fact, studies indicate those young women who do not have their natural fathers in the home will actually hit puberty earlier than normal. My guess is that this is partly a bodily response to not feeling loved by her father in her earlier years so the body actually works to be more attractive in the adolescent years. If you truly understand that without affection and touching you will die emotionally, then you'll understand why so many young people are getting involved with pre-marital sex.

I also have a word of advice for stepparents today. You, even more than biological parents, must learn to communicate with your stepchildren in a non-threatening way. If you're going to have a good relationship with them, you will have to be affectionate, hug them, and encourage them, but also respect their space. Don't be hurt if they push you away for a while, just keep acting in love. Don't be harsh with them. Remember, they didn't choose you, you chose them. Don't expect them to immediately accept you as their new parent. That is a relationship that will have to be built piece by piece. Learn to talk to them and listen to them. Make communicating with you a safe place to be so that after a while they can come to you on their own because they know they will always find love, affection, and help when they are around you.

LEARN TO LISTEN

Most people have their own agenda in any conversation. They have what they want to say and all they want people to hear is what they have to say. Most of us, particularly we men, are not good listeners. We might be good talkers, but are seldom good listeners because it takes energy to listen—especially to what may not be central to the way we think or approach issues. We tend to lose interest fast when the issue under discussion is not really relevant to the tasks our mind is working on at the time.

> If I could give any husband a word of advice, it would be to ask his wife questions in every discussion.

If I could give any husband a word of advice, it would be to ask his wife questions in every discussion. Forcing yourself to engage so that you have good questions to ask is a first step in listening, and then we tend to be more interested if we are listening to answers to questions we initiated. Keep the questions casual, centered on getting to the heart of what she is talking about, and affectionate. Don't let it turn into an interrogation. We have to be careful that we don't talk to her like one of the people we manage at the office—it is often easy to fall into your work pattern when you are at home and treat family members like employees.

~

Courage is what it takes to stand up and speak;
courage is also what it takes to sit down and listen.
Sir Winston Churchill

~

One thing I've learned about women is they want you to listen. It affirms them. But because most men try to fix everything, they listen to a little bit, and then try to fix whatever issue their wife is discussing. This, again, is a work pattern—we fix things all day at work and then want to stay in that same pattern at home. This is a bit demeaning, though, because if we are always trying to fix their problems we are treating our wives as if they are incapable. The same can be true with our kids. If Dad always fixes everything, how will they learn to fix things themselves?

Most women don't want their husbands to fix everything. As they talk, they are working on the problem themselves. They just want you to listen. Your love and affection expressed in listening gives them energy to handle the problem on their own.

Key #7
Effective Communications Starts with Listening.
Only Work on Your Responses
Once You Understand What
She Is Really Saying

As I have said before, I get up first in my house, fix the coffee, and am off to work in my home office often before my wife is even up. She is a night person and I am a morning person. However, when she is up and has had a sip or two of coffee, she wants to be social, so she comes to my office and sits down to chat. At that moment, I always have a choice which never seems to get any easier: I can either stay focused on whatever it was I was working on when she came in, or I can choose to engage with her and listen. I have to admit, I don't always succeed in choosing to listen, but I do think I am getting better with practice. I have found it best if I turn to focus on her, keep my hands away from my computer keyboard or something else to fiddle with, look her in the eyes, and ask questions. She needs to know that she is the most important thing in my life, and I have found that sincerely listening during these little morning times is one of the best ways for me to communicate that.

Men, we need to realize that we have incredible con-
centration skills that, if not overridden, can tune literally
anything out. We can lock into any task (particularly if it
involves a TV screen, a car engine, or sporting event) and
not hear a thing that happens around us. I don't know
how many times I have missed what my wife said while
the TV was on and commercials were playing at the time!
We tend to naturally focus on the visual stimulus more
than the auditory, but it communicates to our wives that
we care more about the TV than we do about them!

We all have a need to be number one in our mate's
life. If we don't listen, it communicates that we don't care.
That's why we must slow down and listen, so they know
we care.

Now notice that I am focusing on you listening to your
wife, while I know there are some of you reading this
whose first thought is, "But she never listens to me!" That
may be true, but you really can't control the other
person, you can only control yourself. With someone you
have partnered with, you can't dictate what happens in
the relationship, you can only lead by example. You can't
make the other person show love to you, you can only
woo by showing love to the other person. This is what
was meant when the Bible said that men should be the
head of the household (Ephesians 5:23) not that we can
dictate to our families as if we were their bosses, but that
we would lead them through inspiration and example.
Too many men want to dictate to others what to do and
then live selfishly in what they do. These men miss the
true power and true rewards of leading their family.

Learning to listen is the first step to becoming an effective leader.

BUILD SECURITY

Men, as the leader of a family, we should provide a place of sanctuary for our wives and children. We provide the safe place to come and express whatever needs to be said. No matter who we are, we all want security in our lives. In our culture today, this is what it means to be the protector of our families more than anything else. I mean, it is not like there are bears and mountain lions roaming around outside of our homes or roving bandits that we need our muskets to defend our families with anymore. Today the dangers are more emotional and influence the decisions our family members make, and if coming to us as the man of the house is not a safe place, then we cannot impact those decisions.

Women still want a home that becomes their nest, even if their work somewhere else consumes most of their time. It's all about security, and the security of the home is defined by the level of trust and intimacy in the conversation of that home.

> Anytime
> there is poor
> communication
> in a relationship,
> people will
> feel insecure.

Anytime there is poor communication in a relationship, people will feel insecure. They will feel like they can't trust the other person with the real issues bothering them, or the real dreams of their hearts. If you want the lines of communication open in your relationships, you have to show them that you support them no matter what. They need to hear you can accept whatever they say without attacking them for it and that loving and supporting them is your primary goal in all of your interactions with them.

∽

In every marriage more than a week old,
there are grounds for divorce. The trick is to find,
and continue to find, grounds for marriage.
Robert Anderson

∽

If your wife gets overlooked for a job promotion, she doesn't need to hear all the reasons why you think she didn't get it. Certainly some constructive criticism may be appropriate at some point, but not while the hurt of the rejection of losing that job is still an open wound. She needs for you to be supportive of her. She needs your sympathy and your love. She needs your affirmation. She needs to know you believe in her no matter what anyone else has to say and that you know there is something better for her out there. Then, perhaps, as she prepares for the next interview, she may ask you what you think she can do better this time, and then you can lovingly share some of your ideas on how she can help her prospective employer see that she would be a tremendous asset to his or her business.

You will never earn her trust in a crisis situation, however, if you don't interact with her acceptingly in the day-to-day situations. Soldiers continue to drill in peace-time to be ready for times of crisis; we need to practice communication in the everyday times so that the channels remain open in more intense times. You will never have a secure relationship until you spend time together every day. There is an old adage that says, "Love is spelled T-I-M-E." I'm talking about spending time together as often as possible so you can build security between you and your wife. People spend thousands of dollars going into therapy because they need someone to listen to them who will validate their feelings. We are designed to solve our emotional issues through talking, but that talking should really take place first in the sanctuary of the home.

~

There are no shortcuts to any place worth going.
Beverly Sills

~

If your relationship is in trouble today, it could be because trust is low. If going to your wife to communicate is not a place of security and support, but is instead a place of instability, hurt, and attack, it could be because she doesn't feel your support in the relationship. Even though she may be trying to show you, it may not in ways that effectively communicate it to you. The only way to cut through this is to create a secure environment in which to really communicate, and that security will only come when you are willing to listen first and respond later. What she says may strike a cord in you, but you need to be willing to hear it all out before you respond. Sometimes the trust bridge between you two is so burned though that you will need help doing this. Getting counseling help is not a sign of weakness when this happens, but a sincere gesture of love that you want the relationship to survive and are willing to get help to make that happen. It can be a new way to show your support of your spouse and rebuild those bridges of trust.

Anytime you are supportive in a relationship, it makes the other person feel safe. People get depressed when they don't feel supported, and they don't feel secure in their relationships. When another woman walks down the hall and you are breaking your neck to look at her, it makes your wife feel insecure. If a husband is criticized for not making enough money, it makes him feel insecure. In either case, the spouse is undermining the very thing they are after.

COMMUNICATION IN LOVE MAKES ALL THE DIFFERENCE IN THE WORLD

When you listen and are affectionate, it builds security in your relationship. When you touch her face or hair, it builds security in your relationship. When you compliment each other, it builds security. The tone of your voice either communicates approval or a lack of approval. Your body language either accepts someone or pushes them away.

When you call your wife in the middle of the day just to see how she's doing, it builds a sense of security within her. She likes to know you are still thinking of her when you are apart. When you take the time to be romantic, it builds security. When you cook her dinner and spoil her with flowers, it builds security. When you take the time to tape a note to the mirror, it says she is number one in your life and it builds security. Even if you have been married for a long time, it's never too late to build security in your lives together.

If you're not supporting your spouse properly, it's only a matter of time before she pulls away from you. Each failed opportunity is like placing a brick between the two of you and mortaring it into place. If you let it go long enough it will be a wall that is difficult to tear back down. If you give her the message that she can't do anything right, it's only a matter of time until she will grow so cold to you that you have an ice cube on your hands.

We all do better when we have the security of one special person's love. We all seem to do better when we have the support and trust of that one person we care most about. This is why polygamy never worked. One man and one woman in a monogamous lifetime relationship seems to be coded into our DNA as what is best for all of us.

And if you will learn to communicate effectively, you will have the most important key to living that best in your life.

Chapter Six

RESOLVING CONFLICT . . . COMMUNICATING IN TIMES OF CRISIS AND HURT

If women ran the world we wouldn't have wars, just intense negotiations every twenty-eight days.

Robin Williams

Speak when you are angry—and you'll make the best speech you'll ever regret.

Dr. Laurence J. Peter

There's a story about a man who was a hunter and was always bringing home game birds for dinner. One day he bought his wife a parrot that could speak eleven languages, but the wife got the parrot by delivery, and she thought it was another game bird that was sent home. So she cooked it for dinner. The man came home and asked if she liked the present that he sent her.

She said, "What present?"

He said, "The bird I sent home."

She said, "The bird?— I cooked it! It's still in the oven!"

He said, "Woman, do you know what you've done? That bird could speak eleven languages and cost over a thousand dollars."

She said, "Well, then why didn't he say something?"

> If you're going to be in relationship with anyone, conflict will occur from time to time...

How many disagreements in our relationships come in just that same way? We don't communicate, and before you know it something valuable is plucked, stuffed, and cooked between us. One of us is so hurt we can't even talk to the other any more. We would rather walk out than put the pieces back together again. What looked at first to have been a small rain cloud turned into a hurricane that threatened to blow the marriage or other relationship right off of its foundation.

THE STORMS OF LIFE

No matter who we are, such storms will come in our lives. If you're going to be in relationship with anyone, conflict will occur from time to time either through internal or external circumstances. Even the most trivial of issues can cause major conflicts, and such arguments tend to expose other areas that have been causing friction for some time. The key is to be able to work through the hurt of these situations and use them as an opportunity for your relationship to grow.

~

Many marriages would be better if the husband
and the wife clearly understood
that they are on the same side."
Zig Ziglar

~

Even if you have solid lines of communication open in your marriage, conflict is still challenging. Crises are a time of testing, and even solid relationships will suffer if we are unwilling to take some additional steps. Arguments will start and the longer you have been together the better you will know how to hit each other's weaknesses and drive the smallest of things into a huge blowout. You have to know how to deal with these issues without it becoming a contest of who can destroy the other person the best. I can tell you, that if that is the case, nine times out of ten, we men will be the losers—women just have too much of an advantage when it comes to dealing with emotions.

DON'T FIGHT ANGRY

Anger has been a very helpful emotion in human history. It triggers adrenaline in our systems to temporarily give us extra strength and stamina to either fight or run from an attacker, whether the attacker is a wild animal, an enemy in war, an opponent on a football field, or a mugger in the street. The problem with anger in marriage, however, is that neither fight nor flight will help us in resolving an issue.

The longer you have been married, however, the more your wife will know the hot buttons to push when you are in a fight. The natural tendency of any person is to hurt back when they have been hurt. Thus, if we let things progress naturally in any argument, the best we can probably hope for is an emotional slug out, and the chances are that your relationship will be the big loser.

Conflict is seldom resolved by ignoring it. It must be intentionally dealt with. Yet if the people in the conflict choose to only try to justify themselves by placing blame on others, then they are like the guy cleaning up because of the hole in the roof of his house—they are only dealing with the symptoms and are avoiding the actual problem. However, in the midst of the storm, it is pretty difficult to fix or cleanup anything, so it is best to find a way to sit it out and work on the issues at hand when the weather is more favorable.

~

The aim of an argument or discussion
should not be victory, but progress.
Joseph Joubert

~

You have to find a way that works for you to call a time out. Anger makes us either want to escalate to the point of getting physical or flee from the situation. It is easy to see where Stan Lee got the idea for the Hulk—he probably got in a fight with his wife. Though walking out and slamming the door behind you is the better of the two options, it is no solution to the conflict. You need to find a way to say, "Honey, I love you too much to fight when I am this angry because I know I will say something stupid and hurt you. In fact, I know I probably already have. Can we take a break from this to cool down and talk about this later?" This is not an easy thing to do and it is unlikely that in the heat of conflict it will come out that objectively, but you need to find a way to do it.

It is best to set some ground rules for such disagreements beforehand when things are calmer and more likely to be better received. To have a conversation something along the line of, "I know that we will have a fight sometime about something. It is inevitable. But when we do, I don't want it to be a big blowout that hurts us both so much that it also hurts our relationship. If we do get in such a fight and I start to feel like I am losing control of my emotions, can we take a time out for a bit so that we can come back to it later and focus on the issue rather than hurting each other?"

If you allow conflict to go on for a long period of time, bridges tend to get broken down. In fact, the more conflict is unresolved, the harder hearts become. It doesn't even matter what the conflict is about. If we let it continue with no resolution, it won't take too many years before those bridges feel as though they are beyond repair.

While the tendency to place blame in such arguments is destructive, the willingness to take responsibility to work together for a solution is constructive. To be able to say to yourself, "You know, it doesn't really matter whose fault it is, the real question is, how do we solve this situation?" It wasn't Thomas Edison's fault people had to live by firelight, but he became a hero when he took responsibility for the solution of the problem and invented the light bulb. It isn't a court's fault that there are problems between people, but when it accepts responsibility for finding a solution, peace can be restored.

> The key question is: "Who is willing to work together to find a solution?"

Who really cares who is responsible for the problem? The key question is: "Who is willing to work together to find a solution?"

Decide to be a peacemaker in your family. This doesn't mean always giving in, but it does mean refusing to attack the other person in the midst of the disagreement. If there is disharmony in your marriage because you are always avoiding conflict by giving in, all you are doing is building up resentment in yourself. You are stuffing the hurt, carrying it around with you all the time. On the surface, you may look cool and calm, but underneath you are on the verge of erupting. If you keep that up, someday it will become so much that you lose control and explode.

Never go twenty-four hours without resolving your anger issues with your spouse—even better, never go to bed angry. If you don't deal with anger, it will turn into bitterness, and bitterness can be like the roots of a weed that get into your heart. The deeper it goes, the harder it is to get out. Just like a weed, if you miss even a little piece of that root, the whole plant will grow back again.

When conflict arises, don't ignore it. Deal openly with your spouse about the issue. Whether you are the one offended or you are the offender, be the peacemaker who will take responsibility to be part of the solution and remember, don't try to solve the problem when you are angry.

If you're going to be a peacemaker, you also need to choose the right time to discuss the problem. If there are sensitive issues, you need to be able to find the right time and atmosphere to discuss them so things won't heat up again in the midst of the discussion. You don't want to drop a bomb on someone, and then leave for work. Timing is crucial. Make sure you have time when you're not tired or rushed to sit down and talk things through. Make sure you are in a place you will not be interrupted. Unplug the phone if you need to, but choose a time where you can talk freely, not be interrupted, not be hurried, and deal with the issue.

BE CAREFUL WHAT YOU SAY

Anytime we have conflict in relationships, we tend to attack the other person. But if we're going to resolve our conflict, we have to attack the issues instead of each other. If you're not careful, your anger will cause you to be abusive in the way you speak to your wife. You have to decide beforehand that abusive, attacking language will never be the way you can resolve any issue. It is not about winning the fight, but about working together to attack the problem.

~

The real art of conversation is not only to say the right thing in the right place, but . . . to leave unsaid the wrong thing at the tempting moment.
Dorothy Nevill

~

Men, we have to acknowledge that we love to intimidate. A major part of sports that makes any game fun to watch is to see if one side can intimidate the other into submission or to trash talk them into losing their cool and the game. That works because the relationship between the two sides is adversarial. Only one can win. However, in any marriage, when one wins, and the other loses, the relationship will always be the big loser. If you're going to resolve conflict, you cannot use anger and be successful in finding a solution where you both win, yet if you don't find a win-win solution you are just setting up bigger blowouts down the road.

Stay away from hitting hot buttons when you fight. Never, and I mean *never*, threaten your partner with divorce just to win an argument. Never attack your wife as a person, as a mother, as a lover, or in any other way.

Never use foul language. If you do, you may win the battle, but the war will just have begun.

The issue may be, however, that you are still insecure about who you are. If that is the case, when arguments come, you will react by trying to make the other person seem smaller than yourself. If you find yourself doing that time and again, it is time for you to do some self-examination and get things straight. If you find your wife doing that to you, then you need to find a way to build her up and give her the confidence she needs to believe in herself.

You'll never be persuasive when you're abrasive. Men what do you call your woman? Do you call her sweetheart or do you call her stupid? Do you call her pretty or do you call her ugly? Do you call her the apple of your eye or do you call her fat? When you married her, you became the most influential person in her life: are you going to use that influence to build her up or tear her down? If you are going to tear her down, you have to realize that all you are doing is attacking yourself.

If you will brag on your spouse, she will become what you call her. If you will build up your spouse, she'll never be looking for approval from another man. If you will brag on her, she will do everything possible to live up to what you say.

DEAL WITH THE ISSUE

Surrounding any issue we face, there are always a lot of side issues that can be distracting. As we touched on earlier, as individuals before our marriages, each of us has baggage of our own from how we were raised, the stability of our childhood families, past relationships, or any number of other things. As single people, those issues can be relatively easy to let slide. We live in a cloud of self-delusion that we are a pretty good person. If we didn't, we would probably never have enough confidence to get out of bed in the morning.

When we are dating and in the early years of marriage when our infatuation with each other is still strong, our issues are still being glossed over, and we can continue like that for years while the pressures of our relationship are low and things seem to be running smoothly.

However, marriage tends to triple the effect of these issues. Now, there are not only my unresolved issues, but also her unresolved issues, *and* the issues that we let develop between us by never dealing with our own weaknesses. A leaky pipe never really causes trouble if there is very little water pressure running through it.

Now bring in a crisis, and what happens? Suddenly all the issues from the entire marriage we haven't dealt with burst out. Under the increased pressure, the leaky spots in the pipes burst. Just like in the story of the house with a section of the roof missing, as long as there is fair weather or only light showers, it is really no big deal; but just let a storm come and the entire house is flooded.

In the midst of a crisis, the issue can easily turn into "You never . . ." and "You always . . ." Little issues that have very little to do with the crisis at hand can explode into the forefront and blind both husband and wife to the real issue. Small frustrations, like leaky pipes, explode with emotion and words are said that cut deeply. Suddenly instead of the one crisis, you have half a dozen and it feels like your marriage that was coasting smoothly through good weather is on the verge of sinking in rough weather.

~

A smooth sea never made a skilled mariner.
English proverb

~

This is one of the reasons why, when you have small conflicts, you shouldn't try to sweep them under the rug. You have to face them head on while they are still small enough to handle easily.

Be honest with yourself. You are not perfect. There are things you can do to handle your baggage in such a way that it is either resolved or out in the open so that it doesn't blindside either of you in a time of crisis. Such humility will not only help you, but your intimacy with your wife will improve as well. The old saying, "A man who loves his wife, loves himself," is true at several levels. Every wound you inflict upon your wife will ultimately be your own.

> If you can never learn to defer to your wife's strengths, you will always suffer for your weaknesses.

Marriage is a lifelong process of overcoming differences, building trust, and compensating for the other person's weaknesses. If you can never learn to defer to your wife's strengths, you will always suffer for your weaknesses.

When people say that they are incompatible, they are really saying the either one or both of them are just too selfish to be honest about their own faults, to deal with them, and to make the changes necessary to alleviate them. Most of us have issues in our lives, but often we blame the other person. We are not prepared to make sacrifices to change ourselves. Our problem is that pride comes in and makes us think that we're okay when we're not. If you can admit that, there is hope of humility enough to grow. If not, you will be facing even tougher waters ahead.

Again, as men, we need to take the lead. Remember, stick to the issue at hand in the midst of any crisis. Don't give in to the temptation to bring up side issues about her even if she gives in to using this as an opportunity to rake you over the coals for your shortcomings. I know that can be pretty hard to do, but if things get too emotional, you need to be able to shut the hurt down enough to deal with the real issue. In such cases, you have to go back to your agreed upon method of calling a time out and come back to the issue when you are both less emotional and better able to stick to the crisis at hand.

AVOID FRONT-ON EGO COLLISIONS

When you go head-to-head with your spouse, espe-cially after you have been married for a while, you get to know the hot buttons that will drive her into a frenzy if you push them. It is tempting that when she says some-thing that really hurts you to turn on her, hit those buttons, and enjoy the show of her hurt in retaliation for yours. We choose to go toe-to-toe/ego-to-ego and want to slug it out until one of us wins with no consideration for the other person at all. These tactics may win you a few battles, but will ultimately lose you the war.

If you're going to heal conflict in your life, you must understand your wife's perspective and let her be rational as well. Don't hit her below the belt so that she gets so angry that she just gives up. Let her find a place of secu-rity from which to honestly express herself and then sin-cerely listen to understand her viewpoint to see if you can see it the way she does.

The root of all evil in the world is really selfishness, and selfishness is really just unbridled ego. It blinds us to the needs of others and makes us feel justified in doing whatever we want from belittling others, to theft, to murder. It blinds us to our own shortcomings and to the fact that ultimately what is best for us is what is best for our loved ones, even if it requires self-sacrifice in the short term.

The secret of resolving conflict is in understanding where the other person is coming from, what is best for them, and then what is ultimately the best for both of you together. It turns you from adversaries to allies, and the power of two that are unified together is ten times that of one of you alone. When we make an intentional shift to look at the other's needs, it helps us in handling the conflict. Anytime we understand where our wives are coming from, it's much easier to resolve the issue between us.

~

Marriage is the operation by which a woman's vanity and a man's egotism are extracted without an anesthetic.
Helen Rowland

~

To do this, we have to put a harness on our desire to defend ourselves and rein it out of the way. Otherwise, while she is speaking, all you will be considering is how to justify yourself in response and you will really hear nothing of what she says.

If you are going through conflict today, chances are that you're angry. When you're angry you're preoccupied with yourself, but when you put the other person first, it helps you get your mind off of yourself. In a marriage relationship, you must be willing to make adjustments and be flexible. If you're going to handle conflict, you can't always have things your way. You have to be willing to put yourselves as a couple before yourself as an individual. Only when you do that will you create resolutions to your conflicts that will build your marriage instead of tearing it apart.

CHOOSE TO FORGIVE

The most likely thing to block you from connecting with your wife and being able to truly resolve issues together is your inability to surmount your own hurts. When you leave the bricks of poor communications and past issues between you, you will have trouble communicating through that wall. Honestly forgiving your mate—and sometimes yourself—is the only way of knocking that wall down to restore your relationship.

~

Unforgiveness is like drinking rat poison and then sitting back to wait for the rat to die.
Anonymous

~

If you are going through conflict today, one of the first things you have to do is to be willing to forgive. We tend to make two mistakes when it comes to forgiveness: 1) that the other person needs to apologize or somehow make it up to us before we forgive them, and 2) that forgiveness is only for the other person.

People often get offended without the offender even realizing it. We are offended when others are callous towards us, or when they say things they may not even really mean. Quite often they don't even realize that what they said has hurt us, then we grow bitter towards them and they aren't even affected. Regardless of that, the bitterness grows in us and hurts us more and more as it is fed through other interactions where we are again offended. The only way out of this self-destructive cycle is to forgive the other person regardless of whether they ever ask for forgiveness.

Key #9
When You Come to The End of Your Rope
Choose to Respond in Love And Forgiveness
It Is Your Only Chance to
Get What You Really Want

Anytime you are going through conflict, you need to concentrate on reconciling before you can concentrate on resolution. There's a very big difference between these two. Reconciliation means to reestablish the relationship. Resolution means to resolve the issue. It is quite possible to resolve the issue and leave the relationship in tatters. Keeping your relationship intact and both of you united against whatever comes is far more important than solving every problem you face the way you want it solved. Whether you realize it or not, you are not going to resolve every issue. We are not going to come into agreement on everything, but no matter what, we can love each other.

Because we are different people and different genders, we will never see everything exactly the same way. Because each of us has a different perspective, we will see things from a different angle. If we are willing to listen and share with one another, this can be an advantage rather than a disadvantage; if we are not, we will more often than not find ourselves on different sides of the fence. We need to realize that disagreeing doesn't mean somebody is right or the other person is wrong. It just means we have two different perspectives to consider together. You're not going to agree with everything your mate believes or thinks, but you can disagree without being disagreeable. If you make the conscious decision to, you can walk in unity without agreeing on everything.

Don't let anything come between you. You will never have a successful marriage unless you learn to forgive and let go of the hurts. If you hold on to the hurts in your relationship, they will only grow worse, and they will hurt you more than anyone else. Unforgiveness is like a poison that kills marriages. Get it out of your system as quickly as possible.

If you hold grudges and are bitter, it will kill your relationship. The moment you refuse to forgive, it will create a hidden conflict in your relationship that will start to grow. Although we want to hold on to the hurts to use them later as ammunition, we must not harbor and nurture these little offenses to be used later. If we keep score against our mates, our marriage will suffer for it. The only right thing to do is forgive.

~

That married couples can live together day after day is a miracle that the Vatican has overlooked.
Bill Cosby

~

BE WILLING TO ASK FOR HELP

If there is conflict in your life, you need to know that you are not alone. A lot of times we get into trouble because we didn't do something we didn't know to do. In other words, there are things we could have done to avoid the situation, but since we didn't know what they were, we didn't do them.

> Realize that if you didn't know how to avoid the trouble you are in at present, it is also unlikely that you will know how to get out.

We live in a society, however, where helping others is valued. If you are a member of a church or other community of faith, then there are people there ready to help you, and if they can't, then they will likely know of someone they can direct you to. That is always the best place to start.

If you are in a financial crisis, seek counseling from a financial expert. If you are in a medical crisis, seek a doctor. You may need legal advice in a situation. Realize that you are not the first person in the world to face any crisis and that someone out there has been through it before, and that they can help you survive it as well.

However, some are too stubborn or too embarrassed to ask for help. Realize that if you didn't know how to avoid the trouble you are in at present, it is also unlikely that you will know how to get out. It may also be that the communication bridges between you and your spouse have been so completely destroyed that neither of you trust the other enough to start the repairs. An outside neutral party is your best bet. There is safety in getting external help that you may never find with just you and your spouse. If your marriage is important, then it is worth asking for that help.

However, with that said, be sure when you ask that you are open to the solutions they present. I know too many people that will go from counselor to counselor looking for the answer they want rather than the solution presented. Accepting help can be a blow to the ego because we may have to change the way we do things. We may have to admit we were wrong. Don't go to counselors looking for justification. Go looking for what changes you need to make so that your relationship stays healthy and thrives.

People who have been living on the wrong kinds of food and little exercise have some serious changes to make if they have a heart attack and want to avoid a second one. People who buy whatever they want on credit whenever they want it may have some serious belt-tightening to do if they are ever going to have enough money to retire. If we get into crisis because we acted one way, then it is very likely we will have to change some behaviors to get out of the crisis and keep from repeating it. There are always growing pains between levels in life; we need to be willing to bear through that pain or the next level will forever evade us.

PEACE STARTS TODAY

If your home is a war zone, you need to make some changes today. Everyone needs to make up their mind that from this day forward, they're going to resolve their conflicts peaceably, that their relationship will always be the winner, and that they will make every effort to listen humbly without letting emotions and selfishness get in the way.

Homes are meant to be sanctuaries from the dangers of the world, not war zones that force us into the world to find satisfaction and solace. From this day forward, we need to make up our minds that our homes are going to be places of peace and safety. As men, we need to determine that the safest place for our wives and children to come with any problem is to us. We need to decide that we will not retaliate against our loved ones when what they say shocks or offends us, but that we will resolve our conflicts peaceably, no matter how painful it is at the moment.

If there are issues or hurts that are dividing you and your spouse, reconciliation is really nothing more than letting go of the past and choosing to forgive. Even if you have been hurt, it's time to let it go. Forgiveness is really nothing more than letting go of the past.

Improving your communication skills will solve a whole lot of your troubles. The words from your mouth are like the bit in a horse's mouth—they will guide you to victory or guide you to defeat. What are you saying to your spouse or girlfriend? Don't ever let anger control what you do. Don't let the sun go down on your anger. We men get our pride hurt and so we don't want to talk anymore, but it's the worst thing we can do. You hug one side of the bed, and she hugs the other, and—oh Lord!—don't anybody try to slide their foot across the middle of that bed!

Hurts happen in relationships, but they don't decide the future of the relationship unless we decide to do nothing at all. You've got to make up your mind that from this day forward, you're going to treat her differently. You're going to talk to her differently. From this day forward, you've got to let go of all the things she did to you and ask forgiveness for things you did to her. You can't go forward unless you let go of the past. You cannot bring healing into your relationship until you let go of all the injustices that have happened between the two of you.

If your relationship is in a mess today, it's not too late to turn it around, but you need to say, "From this day forward we're going to handle our conflicts in a different way. From this day forward we're going to talk through our issues. We're going to talk about the things each of us has done to hurt the other. From this day forward I forget the past and choose to move on."

~

But now ye also put off all these: anger, wrath,
malice, blasphemy, filthy communication
out of your mouth.
Colossians 3:8

~

You can't change what people have done in the past, but through forgiveness, you can be released from the pain.

The memory may stay with you, but the pain goes away when you choose to forgive. If this is going to be your year, then you have to handle conflict in a different way, and there is no better time to start than the present.

Chapter Seven

TEACH ME HOW TO LOVE YOU

Do you know what it means to come home at night to a woman who'll give you a little love, a little affection, a little tenderness? It means you're in the wrong house, that's what it means.

Henry Youngman

Those who love deeply never grow old; they may die of old age, but they die young.

A.W. Pinero

L ove is like a seed, sunshine, and water all at the same time. It is something that you plant in the life of another person, water with your words and affection, and then shine upon with your encouragement and appreciation. Doing any one of these alone is not enough to nurture love until it grows to the point of giving fruit back to you. If you do this right, you can enjoy that fruit for a lifetime.

There is a proverb that says, "He who loves his wife loves himself." In others words, if you are loving and giving to your spouse, ultimately you are loving and giving to yourself in what you will receive back from a happy, fulfilled, and overflowing-with-love woman. It is all too true, but far too few put it into practice.

Many men will give love, affection, and appreciation to a woman until they get the "first fruit"—and then they are ready to move on to another. They think sex is the only benefit of this process, but they soon find their lives empty of any real satisfaction because after a while, even these acts of conquest lose their thrill.

Others, who are smarter, will save tasting that first fruit until marriage. But then they somehow assume that their wives will flourish just because they are near them, so they think they can turn off the water, sunshine, and nurturing. After a while, when the fruit becomes more scarce, they start to fight about it hoping to squeeze more out of their wives—without having to put any more into them. Then, after a few years of this kind of treatment their wives leave to look for a better farmer who will really take care of them, these surprised men wonder what happened and can't believe their wives would be so self-centered.

A good husband, like a good farmer, knows that everything he gives into his wife will be multiplied back to him several-fold if he will just do it consistently, patiently, and in the right ways. A good husband also learns the uniqueness of his wife, studying her as one of his most interesting subjects, and learning to love her in the ways that feed her the best. He knows that everything he invests will give years of return in the future, so he joyfully loves his wife as if he were building his own business or drafting and managing his fantasy team online. Why? Because he knows that if he does it right, he can turn fantasy into fantastic, and dreams into reality!

Now I don't mean to be cold and calculating about this because, of course, it can't be done without real heart, but I do want to emphasize that with current divorce rates, we men must be doing pretty poor jobs of caring for our homes and gardens. Fruitful marriages— and I am not talking about how may kids you have!— seem few and far between these days. When was the last time you were with a married couple and you felt inspired because they seemed so full of trust, confidence, and giving toward one another that it overflowed to those around them? If it has been a while—or never!—then you know what I mean. And even if it was recently, how many couples like that do you know? If it is more than two or three, then you are extremely fortunate—or else living on a 1950s television stage set!

LEARNING HER LANGUAGE

In his bestselling book, *The Five Love Languages*, author and marriage counselor Gary Chapman states that each of us respond to love in different ways, and while each of us is unique in the exact dialect of love that we respond to best, Chapman found that all of us tend to fall into one or two of five major love-language families. These groupings are: 1) quality time, 2) words of affection, 3) giving and receiving gifts, 4) acts of service, and 5) physical touch.

~

*Ever since Eve gave Adam the apple, there has
been a misunderstanding between
the sexes about gifts.*
Nan Robertson

~

What I want to convey here is that sometimes we
think that we are loving our wives with all of our hearts,
but the message she is getting is something completely
different, especially if our love language is different than
hers (and it usually is—just as most of us are attracted to
our opposites in marriage, we are also usually attracted
to someone who "speaks" love differently as well). This
is why you have to study your spouse in the same way a
farmer studies the soil, the types of plants he specializes
in, the weather, and whatever else he needs to know to
get the best crops. If we want the healthiest, most beautiful, and most thriving wife, it will take some thought and
wisdom.

Too many of us think that marriage is the graduation
ceremony from Wife U. I mean, we think if we can catch
'em, we pass with flying colors and the rest is downhill.
But remember, graduations ceremonies are called "com-
mencements," because they are beginnings, not ends,
and that you don't enter the "real world" until after you
graduate and find a job. Graduating from college is great,
but if you stop there you will never really accomplish
anything outstanding in life. In the same way, winning
your wife's heart enough for her to say, "I do," is also fantastic, but real life isn't a movie—it doesn't end at the

wedding. Getting married is really only the beginning. You have passed the application and interview process, now it is time to get down to work.

Or maybe it's better that we take some refresher courses and work on our masters and doctorates. After all, we don't want anyone else to become specialists in the area of loving our wives—and the chances are that if we don't, somebody else will!

Now I don't mean to draw a cold parallel between our marriages and pursuing our careers, but the truth of the matter is that you still only get out according to what you put in. If you don't like what life is giving you, you've got to make some changes in what you are giving out with your life. As men, we should be so giving to our wives that they cannot resist our love. In order to do this, however, we need to study our wives and learn what best expresses love to them—otherwise we will never build in them the confidence they need to feel they can give back to us. If we choose instead to tear at their confidence and try to squeeze only what we need out of the relationship, we are ultimately creating a void in our marriages that sucks the life out of us instead of revitalizing us.

> If you don't like what life is giving you, you've got to make some changes in what you are giving out with your l

FILLING THE "LOVE TANK"

In life it is as if each of us has an energy core that is fed by love, positive experiences, accomplishment, entertainment, and whatever else motivates and inspires you. Author Gary Chapman calls this our "love tank," and Stephen Covey calls it an "emotional bank account." Whatever you want to call it, however, it is as if each of us has a place inside of us—in our hearts, if you will—where we either store up or subtract away from the love and affirmation we each receive in life. This either energizes us to do well or becomes a void inside of us that can become something like a black hole, selfishly sucking from the world anything positive that gets in our range. I am sure you know such people who, when they walk into the room seem to dry up every ounce of joy from the atmosphere. While most of us operate somewhere in the middle, the goal of every husband should be to fill up his wife's love tank to the point that she is constantly running over and filling him back up as well.

In order to do this, however, we need to understand that there are different kinds of love. There is a love that is uncontrollable such as "falling in love" or reacting to a beautiful woman who makes us look twice or arouses lust within us. We often dilute the word love with things that give us pleasure, such as "I love pizza" or "I love baseball" or "I love Nascar", but the kind of love that we need to fill our wives' love tanks with has to be more intentional and more selfless. The world says that love is butterflies, warm fuzzies, and a knot in your stomach, but I say love is the way you treat each other—love is the way you meet the other person's needs. Love is an attitude of "I am going to be a blessing to you no matter what."

Marriages deteriorate because of what you might call a love tank downward spiral. We get into a situation where we feel like we need love, so we draw on it from our wives without giving back, then when they feel needy for love and affirmation they try to extract it from the us to fill themselves back up, then we feel more depleted than ever and the cycle goes on, with each trying to squeeze the love they need out of the other, but no one giving back. This happens because of insecurity, which is really just the fear of rejection gone to seed. This makes us want to reject the other person before they have the opportunity to reject us.

> Marriages deteriorate because of what you might call a love tank downward spiral.

Have you ever seen a defensive person? It's because they don't believe they are loved. In fact, they may resent you and take on an attitude toward you when you reach out to them. This, of course, leads to very negative interactions. We put the other down so that we can feel better about ourselves, or we ignore each other and focus on our other "loves" sitting in front of the television, hiding at work, or always staying out late with the guys after a night of playing softball or basketball. Our wives might let their need to talk and take care of details turn into nagging. Fights tend to turn into character assassination

attempts. Negativity and selfishness leads to more negativity and selfishness and the downward spiral can be
bottomless—people either learn to live together and be
miserable, avoid each other as much as possible, sleep in
separate beds, or divorce.

~

*My wife Mary and I have been married for forty-
seven years and not once have we had an argument serious enough to consider divorce;
murder, yes, but divorce, never.*
Jack Benny

~

However, this cycle can only be reversed by someone
deciding to love the other even if no love returns for some
time. This is not easy, but the rewards are always worth
it. The goal is to actively love them until they eventually
overflow with love to the point it spills back over to you—
and then you just keep on loving them like that to the
point that even the smallest acts of love blossom into the
game of trying to out love each other—which I know from
experience is a pretty fun game to play! This will take
some conscious effort as well as wisdom and persistence
in loving your wife just the way she needs to be loved.

Now you may ask, "But why does this have to be the
man who does this? I mean, I have my needs too. Why
doesn't she meet my needs first and then I will be full
enough to start meeting hers?" That could work, but let
me ask you a question: who tends to be controlled by
their emotions more, men or women? Women, of course.

So then, who would you expect to be better able to pull out of an emotional spiral better, men or women? If we are honest, we will see that it is we men who should be the more rational, be able to identify what is happening, and be able to make the conscious decision to perform "acts of love" that will reverse the downward spiral.

In other words, it is time to take responsibility and start courting your wife all over again.

HONEY, HOW DO YOU HEAR LOVE?

Happy marriages tend to happen because the husbands strive for advanced degrees at Wife U. They became experts in the field of how their wives hear love.

Far too many of us make the mistake of thinking our best days are behind us. "Boy, weren't we something when I was the starting quarterback in high school and my wife was the head cheerleader. Those were the glory days! But now look at us! I have a lousy job, three bratty kids, and my wife and I have both put on the pounds." What happened?

> Dating is really practicing the hard part of marriage—being friends with the alien gender.

What happened is that you stopped expecting more. You settled on being the quarterback for the rest of your life, and when you didn't get that scholarship, your dreams of playing pro ball died and you gave up. But you need to know that we are not supposed to have our happiest years in high school; life should get better and better as we go along! Unhappy marriages tend to happen because men drop out before they finish their courses, and as a result miss out on the best that marriage has to offer.

> Key #10
> In Marriage, The Golden Rule
> —Treat Others as You Want to Be Treated—
> does not work.
> You Need to Treat Her in
> The Way She Hears Love,
> Not The Way You Hear It

We are wrong in thinking that a good marriage can just happen naturally, without much effort on either partner's part. Second and third honeymoons should not be so that we can rekindle the flame of the first, but to continue to fan the fire of our love into maturity. Men make the mistake of thinking that dating is only for single people when they are in the pursuit of "the one" they will spend the rest of their lives with. Married people should date—the only difference is that now that you have found that "one," she had better be the only one you are dating! We make the mistake of thinking that dating is for finding a mate, but the truth of the matter is that dating is for finding non-sexual ways of having fun and filling the love tank of the person you are with.

Think about that for a moment. Our culture today seems to think that the best daters are those who can get their dates into bed the fastest, but that is not true. The best daters are really those who make their dates feel great being with them without any sexual pressure at all. Dating is really practicing the hard part of marriage— being friends with the alien gender. Such friendship is not about what happens in the bedroom, but what happens in the family room and together on Saturday afternoons at the coffee shop or the park. Is one of your loves to spend time doing things with your wife? If not, you have culti- vated the wrong parts or your marriage. Just as dessert is always best after a good meal, making love is always better after a romantic evening together when she is overflowing with love back to you. The actual act of inti- macy is easy, but really great love-making happens after years of practice with one woman who can't keep her hands off of you because her love tank overfloweth!

EXPERIMENTAL LOVEOLOGY

In his book on the love languages, Gary Chapman states that while he has seen only five major "language families" of how love is understood, there are thousands of individual dialects within each. In other words, there are special ways of loving your wife that are unique to her alone. Thus day one of courting your wife starts with first determining which overall love language your wife responds to and then continuing the study until you know exactly what makes her feel the most loved.

Too many men do things for their wives to try to make their wives feel loved and then pay no attention to how she reacts until there is a crisis. Think about it for a moment: we all tend to love others the way we would want them to love us—we all speak the love language we learned growing up—but we also tend to marry our opposites—and if they are different, it is very likely that they will "speak" a different love language. So inevitably two loving people will come together and sap each other's love tanks dry not because they are being unloving, but because *they are speaking different love languages.*

~

Life is not holding a good hand;
Life is playing a poor hand well.
Danish proverb

~

The classic example is the husband who says, "I provide everything she needs for herself and the kids, but all she does is complain that I am never home! If I am going to keep providing, I have to put in those extra hours at work! We will never be able to pay for their college if I don't keep putting in these hours! Doesn't she realize that promotions come because I am working so hard for her and the kids?" What is happening? He hears love by being a provider; she hears love by spending time together. In such situations, the more he tries to love her, the more he will drive her away because he is loving her in the way he would want her to love him. Somebody in this situation needs to wake up and smell the coffee burning! You made it for her because you love coffee, but she is a tea drinker and never touches the stuff!

Another example would be the guy who always praises his wife and tells her he loves her, but she is always complaining that she has to cook all the meals and clean up after him. He needs to realize that in addition to hearing his love words, she will hear "I love you" more if he helps with the cooking and cleans up after himself rather than repeating the words "I love you" a hundred times a day. His love language is most likely *words of affection*; hers is most likely *acts of service*; see where the communication breakdown is occurring?

In another home the man might have dinner ready for his wife every time she comes home, but she is upset because he always forgets her birthday or he bought her a lawnmower for their anniversary because he figured she likes to have a well-kept front yard! Get a clue, man! Show some sensitivity! Don't buy her a new set of pots and pans for Christmas because it is practical; instead get her that perfume she likes because it makes her feel pretty. Find out her shoe size and bring her a new pair every once in a while. And don't just wait for special occasions, make them!

It doesn't have to be expensive either. Bring her a flower you picked from your front yard, or take some time this year to find out what kinds of flowers she likes and plant them in the front yard. Leave notes for her around the house where only she will find them telling her how much you appreciate some special quality about her. Listen for when she drops hints about what she wants for those special days and search it out for her. Drop by the local bookstore, buy her a blank card, write her something special in it, and leave it somewhere she will find it while you are at work. Gifts don't have to be big to show her you care, but they do need to be thoughtful.

The old expression, "It's the thought that counts," doesn't mean you got her any old thing because it was a special day, but that the gift shows you were thinking about her and putting some careful consideration and effort into whatever you brought her—thus a poem can say more than a diamond ring for most wives no matter what De Beers tries to tell you.

SHE NEEDS ROMANCE

Learn to romance your wife. It doesn't always have to be soft candle light and a gourmet meal, it can be a long afternoon and a coffee accompanied with, "Tell me your dreams, baby" and an interested ear. Clear your calendar, get a sitter for the kids, and take her somewhere you know she has always wanted to go like an art museum or to a play. It can be clearing out a night of the week to take dancing lessons together—after all, women really like a man who knows how to lead! You may say, "But I don't like museums or plays or dancing." Well, guess what? It's not about you! It's about her! It's about spending time with her and watching her while you do something together that she likes. It is a chance for you to study your wife while her attention is elsewhere. It is a chance for you to observe her while she is enjoying herself.

> Learn to romance your wife.

By and large, most women really don't find it romantic if you clear the schedule for the night, jump in the car, and then say, "Okay, this is your night. What do you want to do?" While they will appreciate the gesture, you have just taken all of the mystery out of the evening. They get more joy out of trying to be figured out. If you have spent the last month listening for something special she has wanted to do or a restaurant she has always wanted to try, and then you say, "Okay honey, I have a surprise for you," she will know you have been paying attention to her. Such attention is worth at least five pounds of chocolates, and the returns are likely to be all the sweeter!

Some people hear love when you call them in the middle of the day, "Hey, baby, what's up?" Others need time alone in marriage. My wife and I do all kinds of stuff together, but sometimes she needs time alone. Now, I don't need time alone but she does. Somebody gave her a horse and so she goes to her horse and she talks to her horse. She combs her horse. She pets the horse. She kisses the horse. She does. This horse is a huge, great, monster of a horse, but she goes up, grabs him, and kisses him right on the nose. That's an escape for her. So I had to understand that she wasn't rejecting me by saying, "Dennis, would you give me a few hours alone with my horse?" She wasn't saying she didn't love me. She was just saying, "You don't need time alone, but I do." Sometimes she gets with a girlfriend and she'll spend half a day doing this or that or whatever, and I have to understand that this is a need she has. The bottom line is, the way she hears love is sometimes, "Leave me alone."

~

Try praising your wife,
even if it does frighten her at first.
Billy Sunday

~

Make it a point to touch your wife often, in a loving manner throughout the day or evening and not just when you want to make love that night. Avoid being a fence-post when it comes to giving and receiving hugs. Put your arm around her and give her a squeeze when you are in the supermarket together, hold her hand when you are walking through the mall, offer her an arm and a cuddle when you are watching TV together with your kids. In fact, kids need to see their parents showing each other appropriate PDA—public displays of affection—because if they don't see it from you, they are stuck getting it from TV and movies, which as most of us know, seems to show the most vulgar sides and tells them that "love" is only expressed through the actual physical act of intimacy! No wonder they are making out in the hallways at school—nobody has even shown them how to hold hands. Kids today think that "hooking up" at parties is a healthy way of interacting with the opposite sex. Men, we need to teach our kids how to relate to the opposite sex through example. We should treat their mothers in public the way we would want our daughters to be treated on a date. Also let them know that the physical act of love-making is to be reserved for marriage. However, this will also have the added benefit of letting our wives feel cherished as we show them affection no matter who is around.

~

The husband who decides to surprise his wife is often very much surprised himself.
Voltaire

~

This also means demonstrating appropriate touching and love towards your kids. I believe that when a child grows up in a family and there's not much loving or touching, they tend to get involved with pre-marital sex at an early age. Any time you see a promiscuous teenager you can bet it's because they don't have proper physical love in their lives. Babies have died in orphanages where they are not held enough or are not played with and given enough attention. When you understand that, then you'll understand why twelve year-olds (and sometimes even younger children) are engaging in sexual activity in our culture today.

Stepparents must learn to communicate with their stepchildren if they're going to have any hope of a healthy household. You've got to begin to hug and encourage and love your stepchildren. Remarriage is a fact of our culture and I want you to know that remarriage is really just an opportunity to do it better this time—that means both with your new spouse *and* your new family. If you're a stepparent, don't try to replace the other parent; just love the kids. Be their friend. Talk to them. Let them know that you're going to be there for them.

Don't act like a dictator to establish your authority; just be their friend. Lighten up and don't be harsh!

GET A CLUE

Americans go through more therapy than any other people in the world. You'll notice if you've ever been outside of the United States, it's not unusual for adults to hug and kiss each other. You go to Europe or Africa and it is not unusual to see two women holding hands as they walk down the street. It's not a perverse thing and it's not a sexual thing. It's not unusual to see men hold hands or lock elbows or hug or kiss each other on the cheek. It's not unusual at all. It's only in the United States that we stick our hand out putting about five feet between us—or we try to hug each other without letting our bodies touch. We look like we are playing "London Bridge" or something!

Another thing, men, when you are in public you need to have eyes only for your wife. Control yourself! Don't ever give yourself a whiplash just because a woman in a short skirt walks by! I mean, there is a difference between a look and—*a look*. Believe me, your wife will notice! The grass may always seem greener on the other side of the fence, but once you jump over, it is often hard to get back. The best way to avoid the temptation is don't even look, don't let your mind go there, and stay infatuated with your wife. In the studies of marriage, it is best to only have one subject occupying your thoughts; in the instance, your own wife.

This may sound odd, but fight things through together. If you have a disagreement, resolve it, don't avoid it. If things get passionate, stay focused on the issue and resolve it—even if you need to put it aside for a bit and come back to it when things are not so heated. Don't sweep little things under the rug because one day they will explode on you. Learn from the little things that bug her and change those things that don't really matter to you. Don't let fear keep you from communicating, because everything you can't talk about together is just one more step away from being truly intimate with each other.

~

When a husband brings his wife flowers for no reason, there's a reason.
Molly McGee

~

Love your wife by running the business of your family together. Too many men think they should control the checkbook of the family because they are the man of the house while their wife has a degree in accounting! But don't go to the other extreme either allowing your wife to handle everything on her own like she is the parent and assigned to taking care of you. Some husbands

> Be flexible in your decision making and when she is right, don't be afraid to admit it.

"check out" when it comes to handling anything at all relating to managing the household, including major financial decisions. There has to be a balance in sharing responsibilities.

Be flexible in your decision making and when she is right, don't be afraid to admit it. Play off of each other's strengths and have regular meetings about things like finances, planning for the future, doing chores around the house, where you want to go on your next vacation, and where you are going to volunteer together in the community. Rely on her God-given intuition in all your decision making as much as you would rely on your own decision-making process. Find a non-profit or community of faith to be part of together and get involved with those outreaches. Do things together around the house. Find hobbies that you can do together whether it is going on walks, playing mixed doubles, starting a family band, or having other families over for dinner from time to time.

Certainly there will be some trial and error in all of this, but don't let the errors set you back. Take them as learning experiences and opportunities to be all the wiser next time. Your wife will know you are trying to love her even in your blunders. Have you ever seen the movie *Hitch*? If not you should. His extraordinary efforts to do things for the girl he is dating all end up wrong, but the relationship ends up right because he is a man of character and right motivation. He sees romancing a woman as an art form for the sake of making her feel prized and truly loved—something we all need to learn to do with the one woman we love the most, and I am not talking about your mother.

YOU HAVE TO SOW AND NURTURE BEFORE YOU WILL EVER REAP

As I said before, in a relationship that has deteriorated to the point of constant arguments and strife, putting "Operation: Teach Me How to Love You" into effect will not have immediate results. Depending on how empty her love tank is, it will take some time to fill it up again, especially if her love tank has been draining from childhood. It will take her some time to see you are sincere and haven't just simply discovered a new way to manipulate her into making love with you. And men, we need to be honest with ourselves in this—no matter what our primary love language is, physical intimacy is seldom lower than number two or three on our lists. I'll even go so far as to say that if you've a good sexual relationship in your marriage, you are probably more stable than most.

There is something about sexual frustration that leads to bitterness and hostility and unforgiveness; so loving your wife is not a matter of denying yourselves intimate pleasures to show her that you care, it's about keeping your love pouring into her both before and after each act of intimacy. But a word of caution: If you do all of this and then experience a very special love-making time together but then roll over afterwards with hardly a "Good night" before you doze off, she will know your real aim was just to satisfy yourself all along. Instead, you need to stay consistent in being actively loving towards her no matter what and just allow physical intimacy to make it all the more rich and meaningful. Once your spouse knows that you really care, everything's going to change!

~

Intimacy is what makes a marriage, not a cere-
mony, not a piece of paper from the state.
Kathleen Norris

~

A relationship will never be healthy if only one person is getting the love and support they need, but men, it is most often up to us to take the lead in changing such an imbalance. What kind of relationships are you in today? If you're in a dating relationship and you don't have proper support, you need to seriously consider walking away. If your friends don't have your back, I say you need to consider whether they should stay your friends. If you are married and don't have proper support, you're going to have to build trust and begin to communicate to one another how you each hear love. Any time we have the love and support of others, it strengthens us. Any time we feel as though somebody has a problem with us, it will weaken us. It's an undercurrent. If you feel this kind of negative undercurrent coming from somebody else, it weakens you and your relationship to others. Sometimes when you feel the undercurrents, you need to stop and confront them in love. I didn't say confront in anger, I said confront in *love* because the goal is to build strength through relationship. Find out how they hear love.

Relationship issues are among the top causes of major stress in our lives. Negative relationships will shorten your life, so if you want to live a long time, you better work on keeping your relationships—especially your marriage—strong and life-giving. Positive relationships, on the other hand, not only help us survive, but they feed energy into our productivity at work and towards the accomplishment of our dreams and hopes for the future. A unified marriage is an incredibly strong force for finding true fulfillment in this world.

DO YOUR HOMEWORK

If I were going to give you a homework assignment on this, it would be, "Write down a list of ten things that you need in your relationship." If you're single, write down a list of ten areas that you have difficulty with regarding the opposite sex, and begin to clear the road for the relationship you want to have in the future. Begin to make changes now so it will go smoother when you meet that special someone. The more you do now, the less difficult it will be later. Begin to work on your own stuff now. If you're married, there is no better time to start working on these things than the present.

Let's say you have a list of eight, ten, or twelve things that you feel you need in a relationship. Now, take another look at it and say, "Okay, five of these are absolutely essential. There's no negotiation on these. For me to hear love and feel love, I've to have these things. I would like these other five, but they are not absolutely essential."

Now that you have done that and you know how you hear love, put that list away and make a list just like it for your wife. Which needs on her list do you think are the most important to her? How can you address them?

What will you try first? Create an action plan and, well, put it into action.

Keep experimenting with different ways to love your wife and see how she reacts. Eventually, if you are persistent and do this right, she will start being open for the best ways to respond. (For the moment, let's set aside the fact that responding with making love would be universally accepted by all males.) Now you have a chance to set an example for her in communicating how you hear love. Remember what you have on your list and find a loving way to communicate it. Not something like, "Why don't you ever fix something I like? It seems like we haven't had that lasagna since we were at your mother's house last summer," but rather, "Boy, do you remember that lasagna you made at your mother's last summer? That was one of the best things I've ever tasted in my life!" Then listen intently for ways you can love her, and put them into action.

I have found this system to be foolproof, though it will take different amounts of time to work depending on the people involved and what has happened between them. Don't be discouraged however. You need a steady resolve to repair a broken relationship, and we have to be willing to admit that sometimes things are beyond repair and we need to get on with our lives. I mean, if you have been divorced for four years and she is remarried, don't go in and try to get her back! You need to move on and make it work better with someone else.

The question today is this, are you loving your spouse the way she needs to be loved? Think about that. Are you willing to meet her needs? If your relationship is in any kind of trouble, it cannot be salvaged until you are able to say, "I will do whatever I have to do to meet her needs." Successful relationships require sacrifice—plain and simple. You will never be a success in life without sacrifice. You'll never be a success in business without sacrifice. You can't be a success in love without sacrifice. And that means that if you are going to really have a great relationship, you need to be able to love your wife in the way she hears love no matter if she's able to love you back right now or not. If you go into it with that attitude, eventually she will love you back; if you don't, however, you are unlikely to stick with it long enough to see the results.

Make the decision today to go back to class at Wife U and get your post-graduate degree. Learn to master the subject of your wife and become an expert researcher. If you do become "Dr. Love," I promise you it will be the most rewarding degree you have ever gotten!

Chapter Eight

WE SHOULDN'T JUST LEAD WHEN IT COMES TO DANCING . . . THOUGH THAT IS NOT A BAD PLACE TO START

Only one man in a thousand is a leader of men, the other 999 follow women.

Groucho Marx

A woman isn't complete without a man. But where do you find a man—a real man—these days?

Lauren Bacall

If anything has changed in the role of being a husband and father in the last fifty years, it is how men should lead the home. With women taking stronger roles everywhere in the world today, it has set a lot of men on their heels, backing out of the way of more and more aggressive females. Some look at this and shake their heads, wondering if the old order of a man's home being his castle is as much a fairy tale as Cinderella or Sleeping Beauty.

Though our homes have perhaps changed from being monarchies to democracies, the need for a man to be a leader is only stronger because of it. In a home where the man and woman each get one vote, the only way to get anything done is through agreement, so, oddly enough men have the choice of either becoming better leaders, or becoming wimps and letting their wives rule the roost.

~

For a husband is the head of his wife as Christ is the head of his body, the church; he gave his life to be her Savior. And you husbands must love your wives with the same love Christ showed the church. He gave up his life for her....
Ephesians 5:23, 25 NTL

~

The thing is, though, most women aren't looking to be the monarch of the home. They want to be led, not in the traditional way of the man giving all the orders, but by being included and consulted in every decision and making those decisions together. Perhaps a better metaphor for today is not found in king and castle, but in the ballroom dancing craze that seems to be taking our nation by storm. In such dances, the man leads but does not dominate, and the woman looks all the better for a good partner who knows how to lead well. In fact, if a man knows how to lead well, the woman not only is showcased and made to look graceful and beautiful, but also has that much more fun because her husband is at taking charge on the floor.

We need men today—real men, not wimps—who are not threatened by women—particularly their wives—and who can lead in such a way that their wives and children look all the better for his leadership and enjoy life all the more. To do this, there are a few things we need to pay attention to that our fathers didn't have to worry about as much—but, you know, with greater trials comes greater rewards. Are you up for the challenge?

~

I am not the boss of my house. I don't know when I lost it. I don't know if I ever had it. But I have seen the boss' job and I do not want it.
Bill Cosby

~

If we are going to be the best possible leaders for our families today, then there are five things that we need to do to get to that place.

BE AN EXAMPLE

I don't have to tell you that men today are represented much differently by the media then they were fifty years ago. We've literally gone from *Father Knows Best* to *Arrested Development*. Husbands and fathers in sitcoms today are klutzes, bums, bigots, sissies, criminals, or just plain absent. Dysfunctional families are the laughing stock of the day, and the dads are normally to blame.

Real life doesn't have to be that way though.

Men, whatever change or characteristics you want your family to have will start with you. If you want your wife to learn to communicate with you by shouting with you, then shout at her. If you want her to be reasonable and listen to you, then you need to be reasonable and listen to her. If you want your kids to have integrity, then you had better be extra careful about keeping your every promise to them. If you want them to follow your lead, then you had better have a vision for your family's future worth following and find a way to communicate it to them so that they are inspired to share in it.

The days of dads as dictators are over—and I don't think we are losing anything in their passing. So many men have a wrong concept of what it means to be the head of their house. To be the head does not mean that you dominate your wife; rather, it means that you lead her and encourage her. It means to be the spiritual leader in creating peace and harmony, not the "boss" who yells orders like a drill sergeant.

Men, whatever we want in our homes we must first become in word and in deed. We need to be loving examples of the characteristics and practices we want our families to exhibit. In other words, do your children see you saying one thing and doing another? Is your wife dressing your kids for church Sunday morning and you are already set up in front of the TV to watch the game? If you put yourself first all of the time, that is what they will learn to do as well.

~

An ideal wife is any woman
who has an ideal husband.
Booth Tarkington

~

There are too many young men growing up today with no examples of real manhood around them. There are too many young women growing up without having a real man around the house so that they see a standard of how they should be treated by the males in their lives. They don't get appropriate fatherly affection at home, so when they go out on dates they are willing to do too much to get a little male attention. And the boys don't know how to act because they are getting their information on dating from MTV rather than a dad in the home who treats their mother with tender love and affection. Just where do our kids get the right examples of a loving couple today if they do not get it from their parents? They certainly aren't getting it from Hollywood.

The majority of young people today are living in a home where the mother has taken the leadership role, and over half of the youth in America today live in a single parent home that is headed by a woman. Men, where have we gone?

It is not that women can't be good leaders, but while women have risen in station, men have acquiesced, and the results have been disastrous. It seems to have been God's plan that all children are double-teamed, and that a male and female example was necessary for each to grow up in balance. With the men dropping out of that equation in our society, kids are more confused than ever about when to stand up for themselves and when to give way to others. Every child must have male leadership and male role models to be emotionally healthy. Though single moms are doing a great job today with what they have, our kids are suffering for a lack of committed fathers. We must do everything possible as communities to bring male leadership back into our kids' lives.

~

Marriage is when a man and woman become as one; the trouble starts when they try to decide which one.
Anonymous

~

Though our wives are also adults and need to be good examples to the family, their effects on the peace and harmony in the home is greatly hampered by men who won't be good examples beside them. Without a man's more objective and rational perspective, things can get too emotional and unpredictable in the home; whereas without the woman's nurturing and intuitiveness things can get too stern and calculated. While things are best when both are engaged, it still seems easier for the man to take the lead and keep the home directed correctly than for the woman to take that role. When women try to take that role, we men tend to check out and feel nagged, and the whole household suffers because we relinquish our role rather than embracing it all the stronger because of our wife's initiative. And, honestly, women have their hands full managing all those details, the least we could do is steer the boat and keep things on course.

BE A VISIONARY

Because men tend to be big picture people and women tend to be more detail-oriented, homes suffer without men to plan out the long-term goals of the family. Just as a business needs a plan for its growth and development for the future, so does a family. If you can't visualize it, it is hard to make it happen. Both the male and female perspective is important in this process, but it is more commonly up to the man to have the master plan just because that is the way we think.

～

Success doesn't "happen." It is organized, preempted, captured, by consecrated common sense.
F.E. Willard

～

Or think of it this way if you would like; how can a man be a leader in the home if he doesn't have any plan for where the family is going? In the dance of life, if the man isn't willing to take the lead, toes tend to get stepped on. It is not that women want to usurp control in families, but if the man is not showing the way, how will she ever follow? Order is not brought through chain of command in a family, but through coordinated effort. If a man formulates a plan for the family's future and then discusses it with his wife and lets her fill in the details, order is found in the home without a battle for control. As long as we follow this simple concept, there will be order in the home.

If your child is failing in school, you have to stop and look at the leadership in your home. If your child is destructive, you have to look at the order in your home. If your child is involved in drugs or premature sexuality, you have to look at what is happening between mom and dad at home. If the parents are constantly in disagreement and arguing, then the children will show the same selfishness and probably be out of control as well. However, if the parents are showing respect for one another and self-control in how they pursue their goals, the kids will likely exhibit that behavior.

Key #11
Your Wife Will Never Respect You as
The Leader of Your Family
Until You Give Her A Vision
And A Man Worth Following

While society today has taught women to take more of an active part in how the world runs—which is a good thing, I might add—it has failed to teach them balance. A blame game has gone on to say that men are the problem, but bad things happen because of selfish people not just selfish men. The answer is not to unbalance the equation to the women's side, but to find a way to work together and empower both sides to do what is right together. The problem is that we don't have enough people showing character and integrity. We forget the incredible power of just paying our bills on time, doing what we say we will do, helping others where we can, volunteering to coach and lead youth activities, and just being good dads responsible for our families. If men would stand up to take a part in these things then the whole world would benefit.

~

In a happy marriage it is the wife who provides the climate, the husband the landscape.
Gerald Brenan

~

Anytime we are visionaries of integrity and character, it brings protection to our families. Our kids learn right and wrong from us. When we drop that guard, it is harder for our children to tell the good guys from the bad guys. So when drug dealers or child molesters come to them with the offer of acceptance that kids are not getting at home, they fall into

> One problem is that too many men think the model of masculinity is the drill sergeant or Rambo-commando type.

their traps. When older guys come to our daughters through Internet chat rooms and ask to meet somewhere alone at night, their need for love overcomes their common sense. Anytime men are not fulfilling their loving, moral leadership role, the family is vulnerable to problems.

One problem is that too many men think the model of masculinity is the drill sergeant or Rambo-commando type. They are willing to defend their homes, but they want to do it as if they are taking the beach at Normandy. They want to intimidate everyone in their family into doing right, and end up with rebellion instead. They teach their family members that they are incapable of making decisions for themselves, so when trouble comes knocking, they just say "Yes, sir" in the same way they have been taught to say "Yes, sir" to their fathers. When they learn from discipline that is unreasonable, they run from it when they are in trouble rather than running to it for protection and stability.

Other dads surrender their leadership role to their wives and go and hide at the office and in their hobbies. They spoil their kids to keep them out of their hair. This teaches the kids no more about thinking for themselves than the drill sergeant dads do and the kids know no more about deciding between right and wrong than if it had been shouted at them.

Anytime there's a lack of real male leadership in the home, the children can begin to question their sexual identity. Psychologists say a child gets their sexual identity from the father. When a child doesn't receive male approval at home, it perverts their thinking. Anytime there is weak male leadership, it can cause a young man to question his masculinity or a young woman to question her sexual orientation. Any time a boy sees a dictator dad shouting out commands and finds no desires in themselves to latch onto that kind of masculinity they wonder if they are not better off being feminine. No wonder there are young men today who think they are a woman trapped in a man's body, and no wonder there are women who think they are men trapped in a woman's body. With no reasonable example of real masculinity that is strong, loving, and reasonable, their sexual compass has no true north by which to calibrate their own orientation.

~

If a man becomes everything a woman thinks
she wants him to become
she probably won't like him at all.
Dr. Phil McGraw

~

Women are hurting today because the men won't take their rightful moral places. Women today are leading their families because the men have let them down. Our kids are out of control because of improper male leadership. Women are fed up because the men won't take their rightful place.

Anytime you see an unhappy woman, you can almost always trace it back to an abusive man or an absentee father. Any male can have sex with many different women, but when men take their rightful spiritual place they will say, "I will only have sex with my wife." Any male can produce a child, but it takes a real man to be a father. Any male can be married, but it takes a real man to plan a future for his family. It takes a real man to discipline his children instead of leaving it up to the mother.

If a man looks to no moral code or faith as greater than his own wants and desires, then how can he expect anyone in his family to look up to him? Men listen, if you don't lead your family properly, the police might do it for you. Wouldn't you rather your kids learn right and wrong from you than from the court and prison system?

And let me be honest here; men, what you think you are doing is secret is having a tremendous affect on your family or dating relationships. Today you can get all the pornography you want over the Internet and if you are feeding on it, then it will affect your family as well. Your kids know more about your computer than you do anyway. If you are drinking more than you should, even after everyone else has gone to bed, it will affect your family. You step on people at work to win power and promotions, but then you think when you get home you can be a nurturing and loving husband and father. Too often we fall into pride and think we can handle things no one else can, and then when we fall apart, we wonder what happened. What happened was that we were proud it made us stupid, and we refused wisdom for our own selfish desires and pettiness. Are they really worth your marriage or your family?

The consistency with which you act as a man of integrity and character will determine the stability you bring to your family. The consistency with which you feed your selfishness will undermine it. The more you spend time with your kids, the more they feel safe and loved. The main reason that gangs are flourishing today is because fathers have abandoned their rightful place in the home. If men are not involved in their children's lives, it creates instability. We have a lot of homes today where the father is in the home but is emotionally absent; he is not personally involved in his children's lives. When there is no stability of a father's love at home, the kids go out into the world to find it and latch on to the first counterfeit they find.

Some of you know exactly what I mean because you had fathers who were absent in just this same way. Is that what you want for your kids? If not, then you have to make the conscious decision to change the pattern. If you don't change the pattern, then you are destined to follow the pattern your dad left for you.

MAKE DECISIONS TOGETHER

Anytime you're in a loving relationship with someone, you should want to do everything together, including making decisions. Traditionally monarchical fathers made all the decisions but if we have learned anything from the last century, it is that women have a great deal of good to bring to the decision-making process. Anytime you make an important decision by yourself, it says you feel the other people involved have nothing worth considering. But when you love them, taking the time to talk it through and plan it out gives you another opportunity to do more together and invest in each other's hopes and dreams for the future.

~

Wives are people who feel
they don't dance enough.
Groucho Marx

~

The right kind of man doesn't make decisions on his own. He knows his wife will see things he doesn't and he prizes her opinions. Somehow, intuitively, women see things their men don't. They can't always understand it, but more often than not they are right. If you block her out of such decisions, you will miss that input and make mistakes she could have helped you avoid.

Furthermore, as long as you are making decisions together, it says that you are on the same team—even if the decision turns out to be wrong, you are in it together. If you are making decisions separately, though, it's only a matter of time before you start blaming each other for wrong choices and your relationship will start to fall apart.

...if the husband nourishes and cherishes his wife properly, she will flourish.

I believe the pressures of the world today are greater than they have ever been before. Because of this, there are greater pressures in the home as well, even though it used to be a place of refuge. If we don't make conscious choices to keep our relationship strong, these pressures will continue to eat at us until we are each living totally separate lives.

~

Husbands ought to love their wives as they love their own bodies. For a man is actually loving himself when he loves his wife.
Ephesians 5:28 NTL

~

However, if the husband nourishes and cherishes his wife properly, she will flourish. It is a wise man that sees great things in his wife and lets her gifts prosper the home as much as his provision does. Some men grow intimidated by their wives successes, however, and try to shut them down. Real men shouldn't let that happen. We should want to see our wives and children become all that they can be and plug into their individual purposes and dreams. If each partner is working together towards these hopes and dreams, reaching those dreams will only be part of the joy—the other part will be the working together to accomplish them.

Men, if your wife doesn't look better after you've married her, then you're doing something wrong. Your love and support should show in everything she does.

BE ADAPTABLE

If you're going to build a loving relationship, you have to be flexible. In other words, there will be times when you don't get your way. There will be times that you make great concessions for the sake of your wife. If you're going to have peace in your home, you have to build loving relationships. That means that sometimes when you are not certain your way is right you are going to have to go with her decisions. And then if it goes wrong, you are going to have to hold the line that it was a decision you made together, not her decision alone. Don't let yourself fall into a trap like, "Well, that time we did it your way, and look how it turned out! I wasn't sure about it. I should have known better. Well, next time we should do it my way to avoid that happening again."

~

The man is the head, but the woman is the neck.
And she can turn the head any way she wants.
My Big Fat Greek Wedding

~

You can be sure that if that is your attitude, those won't be the last words of the discussion! You made the decision together to go with what she thought best, you need to stick to the fact that it was what you decided to do as well. Don't pull the rug out from under her at the last minute! You need to acknowledge that you got into it together and that you will get out of it together. Anytime there is fighting in the home, you can bet that all the relationships will suffer.

A lot of people think that once they are married, it is the woman's job to submit to the husband, but the truth is that they really need to submit to one another, only in different ways. Ephesians 5:21 NTL says, *"And further, you will submit to one another out of reverence for Christ"*. This requires being flexible so that you can always put your spouse before you and make sure that she is benefiting from any decision you make. It also means providing a vision for the family that she can plug into, support, and help to make happen. It means that you are a hard worker, a good provider; you have goals set for everything from your next family vacation to retirement to how you will pay off your house and pay for your kid's college education. It means that you are a man of character and integrity that she feels good being associated with, and in whose presence she can shine all the more radiantly.

SUPPORT YOUR WIFE

Anytime we support each other in relationships it makes us both stronger. Anytime we refuse to be selfish, it builds trust and love between us. Have you ever heard the expression, "I've got your back"? It means no matter what, you are watching to make sure nothing can sneak up on the other one and hurt them. Spouses need to have that attitude about each other, but they can't do that if they are thinking more about themselves than each other or if there is a lack of trust.

∼

Let the wife make the husband glad to come home,
and let him make her sorry to see him leave.
Martin Luther

∼

Think for a moment about what the traditional marriage vows say: "For richer or for poorer, for better or for worse, till death do us part." Most of us say this only at our wedding, but do we ever consider it later on? Are they empty words for us, or do we stick to them through the tests of time? Really we are saying, "Whatever I have and you need, it is yours. We are in this thing called life together and you will always be able to trust me. Your dreams are as important to me as mine, and those that we have together are even more important still. I know, no matter what we face, we can overcome it, because we will face it together. We will do whatever we have to do to make it work." We are sort of like two musketeers: "All for one, and one for all!"

BE A MAN

Marriage is not an institution of what can you do for me. It's an institution of what I can do for you. It's about serving the person you're married to. It's a sacrificial service to your mate. Real men aren't intimidated by women and aren't afraid to put them on a pedestal from time to time and make them feel special. That's why you've got to count the cost before you marry somebody. You know that a relationship is healthy when both sides feel unconditionally loved and supported. If you are in a dating relationship today and don't feel the love and support you need, you must evaluate your future together. The truth is that the relationships in your life either strengthen you or weaken you. There's nothing worse than being in a relationship with someone that doesn't support you. If you are single and in a relationship that doesn't strengthen you, you need to consider walking away.

It is bad enough that we live in a world that's constantly trying to bring us down; we don't need those we are in relationship with to do the same. Instead, we need their love and support. If your spouse feels as though you don't have her back, it's only a matter of time before she gets distracted by somebody else. If you are not supporting the person that you're in relationship with, it's only a matter of time until they build walls and isolate themselves from you.

Anytime you refuse to meet the emotional needs of your spouse, you can bet that resentment will come. Anytime you don't support each other properly, tension will build. If your spouse feels insecure about your relationship, you will never have the love together that you really want. You may have the sex, but not the love, and it doesn't take most married couples long to tell the difference.

Chapter Nine

BURIED TREASURE: DOES YOUR WIFE *GOT IT GOIN' ON?*

A good Wife and Health, is a Man's best Wealth.

Benjamin Franklin

If you treat your wife like a thoroughbred, you'll never end up with a nag.

Zig Ziglar

"**H**oney, can I borrow your cell phone? My cell phone battery is dead?"

It is first thing in the morning, and I know that her cell phone battery is dead because she has been talking on it all night. It is dead because she did not plug it in before she went to bed as I have always told her she should do. On the other hand, I did plug mine in and I know that she knows it. Half a dozen responses explode into my head at once:

- "Oh, did someone forget to plug her cell phone in again when she came home last night?"

- "Honey, when are you going to take responsibility for yourself?"

- "Don't you know that people have my cell number and need to get a hold of me throughout the day? How will they reach me if you have my phone?"

- "No! I pay the cell phone bill! I get to keep my own phone!"

- "Honey, who calls you anyway? You just use that thing to be social. Just leave it at home; you don't really need it anyway!"

- "Really? Well, maybe that means we will be under our minutes this month for a change. Why don't you just go plug it in now and hope it will be charged by the time you get back!"

But instead, I say, "Sure! Have a good time at the mall!" and as soon as she leaves, I plug her phone into her phone charger so it is ready when she gets back.

Now, am I a wimp, or am I wise?

LITTLE THINGS MAKE A DIFFERENCE

It's funny how little things like this about our spouses can drive us nuts and trigger resentment over time. In fact, if you find yourself snapping a less than amicable response to your wife over just such an issue, you should recognize it as a sign that you are probably stuffing some resentment somewhere, your "emotional bank account" has gone NSF, or that something else is bothering you that you don't even realize. Another way to put it is that you are running low on "grace"—your ability to accept, within a reasonable margin of error, hurts, affronts, or mistakes by another person without losing your cool. When such little things really get under our skin, it is a sign that we are running low on self-worth and self-confidence, and need to find a way to get our "love tank" gauge moving towards full again.

~

The great secret of a successful marriage
is to treat all disasters as incidents and
none of the incidents as disasters.
Harold Nicolson

~

Now for me, while all of those responses did occur to me, I never really considered any of them because I made the decision long ago not to let those kinds of issues bother me. I decided that I would do what I could to support my wife in every way I could, because I know that I will only get back what love I give. On little things like this, I make sure that I am not making withdrawals from her love tank over things that don't really matter. In fact, I have decided that when it makes sense, to do things her way instead of my own and not just stand on the principle that "It's my way or the highway—I'm the man in the house!"—because, for one thing, I want to support her as much as I can, and for another, far too many women are choosing to take the highway because of unreasonable positions like that one!

Of course, this is easer now than it was at first. There were some attitude adjustments I had to make in order to keep my cool, but I can also tell you again that the rewards are worth it. In a lot of ways, your wife is the thermostat of your house—the colder you make her, the icier the climate in your home is going to be for everyone!

Though I used the analogy of ballroom dancing in the last chapter, I think it is worth discussing again here. Now don't wimp out on me here because I am talking about dancing—if Jerry Rice can ballroom dance on national television, I know it is no sissy sport! In fact, dancing or taking lessons can be a great date activity for you and your wife. If all you can think of to do is go out for dinner and a movie, you need to expand your romantic horizons a bit! A night out social dancing and enjoying holding each other in public can be a great way to make your wife feel loved and beautiful.

∼

To keep your marriage brimming,
With love in the loving cup,
Whenever you're wrong, admit it;
Whenever you're right, shut up.
Ogden Nash

∼

In all steps of couples dancing, it is the man who leads, but the woman who twirls. In other words, it is our job as men to make our partners feel like the most beautiful and graceful woman in the room. However, when you go to a function where there is social dancing, you can tell right way if the men are confident in this role or not. You can tell which couples are stepping on each other's toes because they are not in rhythm with each other. You can tell which couples are confusing their roles and fighting over who leads by how awkwardly they move about the floor or how they hardly move at all.

Men, if we are going to run our marriages right, we need to learn two lessons from this: 1) to confidently lead, we had better learn the steps, and 2) the goal of our leadership must always be to make our partner look graceful and elegant, because that reflects better on us than if we are pushing her around or fighting for control. The best social dancers are not the guys who get everyone in the room looking at him like they are John Travolta in *Saturday Night Fever*, but those who get every eye in the house admiring the woman he is guiding—making her look like the best dancer in the room.

∼

Whoso findeth a wife findeth a good thing, and
obtaineth favour of the LORD.
Proverbs 18:22

∼

HE WHO FINDS A WIFE FINDS A GOOD THING

We need to realize that when we love our wives, we love ourselves (Ephesians 5:28 NTL), and that the better we can make our wives feel about themselves, the more grace and love will be poured back on us. Happiness in the home starts with a wife whose love tank is overflowing and knows how much her husband appreciates and values her. Is your wife free to be a blessing to you, or is she bogged down with the baggage of feeling unloved and unappreciated by the most important man in her life? (And, yes, I mean you, not her father, or her son.)

There is an old Polynesian story that tells of something exactly like this. You see, in the islands of Polynesia at the time this story took place, men paid dowries of pigs, goats for their wives, and, if the wife was very desirable, cows. There was a man on one of the islands named Johnny Lingo. He was very popular and had done well for himself in working his farm. When it was heard that he was looking for a wife, many fathers wanted him to call for their daughters, but there was a young childhood friend named Mohanna whom he focused his attention on. Unfortunately for Mohanna, everyone, especially her father, saw her as ugly, lazy, unproductive, and rather slow. However, being a bargainer, her father decided that he would ask Johnny for two cows for his daughter, but in the end settle for one because he thought even that would be a great price for such a worthless girl.

As expected, Johnny soon came to call on Mohanna's family. When Johnny asked for Mohanna's hand in marriage, her father followed his plan and asked for two cows. Johnny looked perplexed. He rubbed his chin and thought about it for a moment, and then said, "I am sorry sir, but I do not think that is a fair price. Instead of two cows, I think I should give you eight cows as Mohanna's dowry."

Mohanna's father—as well as the rest of the village when they heard—was shocked. Such a dowry had never been paid for anyone before. Most of them thought that Johnny was either losing his mind or very foolish with his money, however, Johnny insisted he knew what he was doing and Mohanna's father quickly and greedily accepted the offer before Johnny had a chance to change his mind. Johnny wasn't about to change his mind though, and went about the village telling everyone what a bargain he had bartered to be able to marry Mohanna for only eight cows!

A short time later Johnny and Mohanna were married and left the village for their honeymoon. They were gone for some time.

When they finally saw Johnny return, it appeared he had a different woman with him! She was so beautiful, articulate, and confident that it took the villagers some time to believe that this was not, in fact, a different woman, but that it was Mohanna! She had been transformed through the love, respect, and recognition that Johnny had given her. When she realized how much he valued and appreciated her, she began pulling her hair back from her face and letting people see her, she stood up straighter and prouder, and then began to address others as equals. When she did this, others realized that she had never been dumb, only shy, and when she emerged from behind her hair and let people actually see her face, she was in fact, quite strikingly beautiful. Everyone began to admire her. What Johnny had seen in her, she had become, and her father grew angry that he had not asked for a bigger dowry for her.

~

Who can find a virtuous and capable wife?
She is worth more than precious rubies.
Proverbs 31:10 NLT

~

Men, when we find that special one we know we want to make our wife, then we need to let her know how much we appreciate her and how beautiful we think she is. We need to realize that we see her in a light no one else ever has—not her family, not her relatives, not her friends, and not even her old boyfriends. There will be some work and there will be a price to pay so that she begins to realize how valuable she is to you and how gifted, beautiful, talented, smart, and important she really is because if *we* are not willing to do it, who will bring it out in her? If we don't, do we really want to let someone else do it instead?

> No one should make your wife feel more valued and beautiful than you do.

No one should make your wife feel more valued and beautiful than you do.

YOU HOLD THE KEYS

Men, I'm telling you, if you love your wife with all your heart, you can unlock treasures that are inside of her. But one of the first steps may be to get out of the mindset that women should only cook, clean, and run the washing machine. Now, don't misunderstand me, if a woman wants to be a homemaker and raise her family rather than be a corporate executive, then more power to her. That is a high calling no one should look down upon, and our families would probably be stronger if fewer women were seeking careers rather than "making homes" with all their hearts. But we have to face the reality that because of economics today, it is not very practical for moms not to work outside of the house, nor do we accept that as a cultural value the way we once did—so we need to find ways to work with it that are not antagonistic.

The problem is that while women are working more away from the house than ever before, they still seem to be working in the home just as much. The husband goes off to work; the wife goes off to work; and when they both come in, he crashes in front of the TV and she starts dinner and her evening chores. Sorry to say it, but men, we need to help with the housework, meal planning, and cooking. If we are not willing to look for little ways to help with this—say, cooking one or two meals a week, being the laundry person for the house, hiring a housekeeper once or twice a month, and/or getting the kids involved in the process in a major way—you can be sure there will be some emotional landmines around the house that you will eventually step on and set off. If she is both bringing home bacon and also the only one frying it up in the pan, how do you expect her to have energy for anything else (you know what I mean, like, around bedtime)?

Key #12
Your Wife Should Grow More Beautiful And Fulfilled Daily Because of Your Love And Nurturing

For me, my wife is my business partner and I am her partner in running our household. I am always looking for little ways that I can serve her and show her love in a way that she will hear it. Considering that "acts of service" is one of her love languages, this is also doubly important.

> Men, we also need to realize that a big part of developing a vision for our family is plugging into the purpose and destiny of our wife.

Men, we also need to realize that a big part of developing a vision for our family is plugging into the purpose and destiny of our wives. As you know, finding these things for ourselves has everything to do with finding fulfillment in life. The same is true of our wives. As leaders in the dance of the home and growing closer together as we grow older together, we need to be sensitive to both her destiny as an individual and her destiny together with us. Far too many couples grow apart these days because they marry young and then find separate careers and life paths that eventually tear them apart. Too many don't see this coming and then come to a place where her promotion takes her to one place and his to another. Suddenly a choice has to be made between her career and his that might have been avoided with a little forethought, but whatever the final choice may be, because of it, down the road regret is sure to come knocking.

Over the years, thousands and thousands of women have sacrificed their dreams to help their men reach theirs, but this shouldn't be! Men, we have let women down, because we have been unwilling to take the proper lead, we have allowed our marriages to lapse into situations where she has to either choose your dream or hers. We should be building both together simultaneously. As I have said before, two visions often lead to division. There are far too many women today left alone to pursue both career and raise their kids because men weren't willing to work their wives' dreams in with their own when planning for the future.

~

That is what marriage really means: helping one another to reach the full status of being persons, responsible and autonomous beings who do not run away from life.
Paul Tournier

~

Yet where multiple visions bring division; unified visions bring multiplication. Human births take place when a man and woman physically become one; in the same way dreams are birthed and multiplied when a man and wife became one spiritually working towards the same end. It is just as important to impregnate your wife with dreams and visions as it is to impregnate her with children—both are important to your fulfillment in life.

While unique and individual visions are very powerful, nothing worthwhile in the world has ever been done without agreement. Businesses grow because they become partnerships; political parties prosper because people support their platforms; and homes are nurturing where there is a bond of unity. What better way is there for you to build a foundation for your children than to make sure their childhood home is more stable than yours was? That doesn't mean there will never be disagreements, only that such disagreements will never be more important than the unity of the marriage. The fuller both of your love tanks are, the easier it is to not turn disagreements into attacks on each other as individuals.

If you love your wife the way she needs to be loved, she will multiply goodness back to you. Your relationship will show it, your finances will show it, your home life will show it, your dreams and aspirations will show it, and quite honestly your sex life will show it as well. Chances are you already have everything you need in life to succeed. But if you are working against your wife because of your own ego and pride, rather than loving her and letting her contribute her part, neither of you will live up to your potential. We spend so much time thinking about how we will invest our money, but how much time and effort do we spend "investing" in our real treasure: our wives?

~

Having a good wife and rich cabbage soup,
seek not other things.
Russian Proverb

~

A wise man builds his wife so that she will build their home. If you constantly belittle her, all you are doing is tearing away at your own foundation. If there isn't nurturing, love, peace, and joy in your home, it is not because your wife isn't creating it there, but because you are not investing enough love, peace, and joy in her.

Anytime two people are building each other up, they will have the kind of marriage that can overcome anything. If you are never home, it says a lot about the atmosphere you are creating there. We only get out of marriage what we put into it. If you put in love, you will get love back; if you give her headaches, oh the headaches she will give back! You will never have anything good until you are committed to investing good things in your wife—then she will overflow with good things back to you.

LOVE, LIKE GOLD, IS MORE PRECIOUS AFTER IT HAS BEEN REFINED

Make no mistake: all love relationships will be tested. You will never know how together you are until some disagreement tries to tear you apart. The bottom line then becomes which are you more committed to: your own desires or your desire to be together? I don't think you can really, truly say that you love each other until you have been through some hard times together and come out the other side stronger for it. It takes real maturity to stick to her when things get so tough that you feel you are losing yourself.

Men are built for strength, but it is best exhibited in short bursts. This is why guys love football. It is all out intensity for a few seconds and then we can rest until the next play. We are built to be warriors that strike one blow and defeat our enemies. If we are not confident in ourselves and don't have some support from outside of us, that strength can seem paper-thin—we are all show and bravado, but when some tough situation calls, we simply fold. We just don't hold the cards we need all by ourselves.

Women, on the other hand, are built for endurance. I mean, if there is anything that makes a marathon look wimpy it is the ability to carry a child for nine months, go through twelve hours of intense labor to give birth, and then nurse that baby every two hours for the next several months. Women can bear hardships and inconveniences that make most of us men feel weak at the knees.

Men, if we want to have that kind of endurance, we have to build up our wives so that they will build us up. We have to let our strength protect and aid them so that their endurance can bolster us. You need to feed her on your visions and let her give you back her ideas on how to fill in the details. Where you have a reasonable plan, she has insight and will see things you never even thought of. If you'll listen to her, she has all kinds of ideas that will help you get to the next level. Remember, you are big picture, she is details—on the surface, you seem to contradict each other, but in unity you complete each other. It is very difficult for a man to reach his potential without his wife's support. When we undermine our wives, we undermine ourselves!

~

Marriage is our last, best chance to grow up.
Joseph Barth

~

Men, we need to be humble before our wives. You need to let her know you need her, but also that you are strong enough to get the job done for her if she will back you up. Unfortunately, though, most men are too proud to admit that they need a woman to help them. We are too proud to admit we are wrong—but I am telling you, it is better for us to admit we are wrong before our wives have to tell us we are!

Men, we are called to be providers, but it will be your wives who will stretch your provision into prosperity if you let her. She can make your dollars cover your needs and then have money left over because she knows where the bargains are. She is the one who will make sure every bill is paid and money is put into retirement and the kid's college funds regularly when you haven't the patience to even sort through the mail. Sure, if you leave it all to her, she might spend $100 to save $30, but if you work together, she will make your budget work. If you don't, you will always be pointing at each other and wondering where the money went!

A wise man will make sacrifices for his wife, because whatever he gives up will come back to him multiplied. Successful relationships require sacrifice just as building a new business does. How many companies have gone bankrupt in the last decade because their leaders weren't willing to make some sacrifices in the executive salaries or benefit packages for a time? Do we think running a family will take anything less sacrificing? When you are willing to let her have her way on issues where she is right or that don't matter, then she will be more willing to follow your leadership where you feel you need to be inflexible for the sake of the family.

~

A man's best fortune, or his worst, is his wife.
Thomas Fuller

~

Too many men, however, need to be right and have their way in everything, and by doing so, all they sow is strife. The more unreasonable you are, the more unreasonable she will be. Men, you can't afford to be inflexible on everything. The more of a dictator you are, the more you feed a rebellion that will one day usurp you and toss you out of your own castle. As they say, "Marriage can be temporary, but alimony is forever." Don't abuse your power because you can't put on a long-term siege the way she can. You may get in the first few blows, but she will outlast you every time. By giving in to your own short-term selfishness, you are sowing seeds of long-term misery; instead you should be sowing seeds of long-term joy and togetherness.

STEP UP TO THE PLATE

Men, it is time we became what we were intended to be. Whether you are just dating, or contemplating your fourth marriage, you want this one to be right—and the only person you can always count on to do what is right is you. And if you lead well, not only will you make your wife love you more and be more beautiful herself, but she will learn to follow your lead and love you all the more for it. It is really up to you: Will you take what you have learned in these pages and bless yourself by being a constant blessing to the woman you love, or will you cut yourself off at the knees and keep failing until you wise up? No matter where you are, the relationship you have now is the best one to fill with a lifetime of joy and satisfaction. Get it right this time—you won't regret what little you have to give to get so much back.

Chapter Ten

WHEN A MAN LOVES
A WOMAN

A man is given the choice between loving women
and understanding them.

Ninon de Lenclos

Happy marriages begin when we marry the ones
we love, and they blossom when we love the ones
we marry.

Tom Mullen

In the creation story before Adam met Eve, God gave
him the job of maintaining the garden and naming all
of the animals. That must have been a lot of work! But
as he had every animal on the earth parade before him,
he must have noticed that all of them came in pairs, and
that he was alone. In the end, he must have realized
something God was trying to teach him: "*It is not good
that man should dwell alone.*" (Genesis 2:18.)

So God put him to sleep and performed the first surgery. It is said that God took Adam's rib to fashion woman from. God could have taken anything, but he took a rib because it signified a place of protection beneath his arm where his wife would rest, and not from his head that she might dominate him, or from his foot that he might dominate her, but that he would be her covering, her provider, her protector, and her lover.

The story also says that God fashioned Eve out of this place near Adam's heart whereas Adam had been made from the dust of the ground. In other words, she was built! She was finely crafted from heart-throbbing flesh, not cold dirt. God meant her to be a thing of beauty, warm, and lovely.

So, when Adam awoke, God told him he had one more creature to name, and He brought her forth. Adam's first words as he gazed on her were, "Whoa! Man!" and the name stuck. She became woman, and then he gave her the name of Eve, probably because he couldn't wait for nightfall!

Since that day, the pattern has stayed pretty much the same. It is still not good for man to be alone, and the first thing we usually say when we see the one we will marry is something stupid. From there the courtship continues until man and wife become one, leaving their families to cleave to each other. They seemed to live quite happily together in that garden for some time. Then there was something about a snake in the grass, an apple, and we have been trying to get back to their ideal life together ever since.

AN ELEVEN-STEP PROGRAM

In the previous chapters, I have outlined what I feel are eleven of the most important keys to living joyfully with the opposite sex. In this last chapter, it is worth taking time to review them more concisely. Believe me, if you understand these and apply them correctly, it will revolutionize your relationship with the women you interact with daily, and significantly impact the way you connect with your loved ones.

Key #1
Women Are Different Than Men—
But, *Vive la Difference!*
Oh, What Fun Those Differences Can Be!

———

We need to realize that women are different from men, and that those differences should be reasons to enjoy life together rather than drive each other up the wall. If we will do a little studying, we can identify some of these major differences, and adjust our attitudes to compensate for them as well as learn to bring each other's strengths out to help our powerful team of two. Just as linemen aren't expected to throw passes and quarterbacks aren't expected to throw too many blocks, we can't expect our wives to always be the logical ones, nor can we rely on our own intuition as much as we trust hers. We have to learn to let her talk so that she will feel loved, and we need to find our "cave time" in ways that won't isolate our families. We also need to learn to trust her instincts for dealing with people as much as we trust our own for getting tasks accomplished.

In the end, if we can't always look to our spouse as our best friend, we are definitely missing out on the potential for the "heaven on earth" that is wrapped up in marriage. Married or single, if we haven't learned that dating has more to do with having fun with your best mate than it does with taking her to bed, then you are missing out on true intimacy. If you can't enjoy treating your wife as your partner in planning and developing your future together, then your future may not be together at all.

~

Marriage is the highest state of friendship:
If happy, it lessens our cares by dividing them,
at the same time that it doubles our pleasures
by mutual participation.
Samuel Richardson

~

Remember that marriage is the highest form of friendship and partnership between two seemingly alien races. Learn the differences between the sexes, learn to communicate across them, learn to laugh about them, and learn the real joy of being one flesh in every arena of life: physically, spiritually, professionally, socially, etc.

Key #2
It Is Not Good for Man to Be Alone, But to Be Desperate to Be with Someone Else Is Even Worse

---

Yes, it is no fun to be alone, but it is even worse to be lonely in a relationship. If you cannot find a way to be happy single, marriage isn't likely to help much either. If you have not found a way to be fulfilled and plugged into your purpose in life, joining your destiny with another will only confuse things further. We certainly can't wait to be perfect before we find the one we want to spend the rest of our lives with—any more than we can expect "Ms. Right" to be perfect, either—but we should at least be able to tell what roads we are on and that our destinations are somewhere out in the same direction.

If we are desperate to find someone else expecting them to make us happy and fulfilled, then we are creating expectations for them that are too high to ever be met. We will also make mistakes because we are too willing to propose to any woman that will have us. We need to date and court women to find out who they are, where they are going, and if our destinies line up or will someday lead us down separate paths. There is a huge difference between "hooking up" and really connecting with someone who will be your soul mate for life.

Key #3
You Can Never Be Your Woman's Man
Until You Are Your Own Man.

———◆———

If you don't know where you are going, how can you ever hope to lead anyone else there? If you don't have confidence with who you are, how do you expect anyone else to? You will never be worthy of the woman you want until you—well—until *you* believe that you are!

Becoming the man you envision yourself to be is very important, but too many want to put off being a man until much later in life or—if possible—to postpone it indefinitely. We need to realize that there is no real virtue in extending childhood, though we also know that forgetting what it is like to be a kid can be devastating as well. But being a real man means almost anything but losing your sense of fun and adventure. Men who are confident in who they are don't have to hide stoically behind some humorless role and become a total dud to be around. Men need to find a place where they can be joyful and share it with those close to them.

You also need to honestly deal with whatever baggage you are carrying from your past. If there is drug or alcohol abuse in your past, get free from that before you join with someone else. If you have past hurts and bad experiences that color the way you see the world, you shouldn't bring those prejudices into your marriage. If your mother nagged you, you don't need to unload on your wife because of it. If you were abused, you need to unpack that suitcase and get rid of it before you have kids. If your dad left when you were young, or could never seem to approve of you, then you need to build confidence in yourself so you can stay the course once you start a family. Burn the trashy magazines and get an Internet company that blocks porn at the server level so you won't be able to dial up those sites anymore. Lighten your load before the honeymoon—there are all kinds of things you don't need to bring with you into your marriage.

If you are single, don't worry about finding a woman. Instead, work on finding yourself and becoming who you feel you should be, then not only will you find the right woman, but she will be attracted to who you are. To adapt a line from *Field of Dreams*, "If you build *you*, she will come."

Key #4
Don't Make Major Decisions about Marriage While "Under the Influence" (Of Love That Is) Balance It by Looking at Her Whole Person

Being in love is great, but it can also make us stupid. We gloss over little points that will later drive us crazy when we are no longer "under infatuation's influence." It can lead us to a point where we one day wake up with a woman we never knew. Don't get your priorities out of whack. To my knowledge there has never been a marriage that has made it solely based on "sexual compatibility" and there has never been a marriage that has fallen apart when it was great in every other area but sexual compatibility. The best foreplay really starts with being best friends. When you have that, the other is easier, but too many put the cart before the horse in this. Find someone who really makes you hum intellectually, emotionally, socially, spiritually, and then you will find the rest is easier to make work.

~

If there is such a thing as a good marriage, it is because it resembles friendship rather than love.
Michel de Montaigne

~

What is she like as a person? Is she vain and selfish, locked into what she can get just because she is pretty, or is there beauty in her life only you can bring out? How is she with money? How is she with friends? Can you trust her? Is she honest with herself? What kind of baggage is she bringing into your relationship? Does she know where she wants to go, or is she just looking for a man—*any* man—to complete her? You need to be able to honestly look at all of this before proposing. If you are already married, however, it is still important to find the answers to these questions and see what you can do about them now that you are together. It is time to go back to school at Wife U and get some advanced degrees in making your marriage better and better each year.

Key #5
You Will Never Find The "Perfect" Mate
But At Least Make Sure The Basics Are
Compatible No Matter What Happens,
You Need to Beware of
The "Relationship Destroyers"

Once you find yourself to be the man you want to be and find a wife who is compatible with your vision and personality, now the real work begins. You are both still human beings "under construction," and now you also have something new to build: a relationship together. Yes, now the real work begins, but also the real joy as well. You have someone with a new perspective to team up with and now you can begin to chase your dreams together, someone to give you honest feedback, and someone to build trust with until you have true intimacy—or what a lot of people refer to as true "into-me-see."

∽

Love is everything it's cracked up to be...
It really is worth fighting for,
being brave for, risking everything for.
Erica Jong,

∽

There is no greater level of fulfillment in marriage than being able to be totally naked with each other—and I mean spiritually, emotionally, and intellectually, not just physically—and still know you are loved intensely. You can't buy that kind of security and trust, you have to work on it together and let it grow between you. Nor can it be achieved once and then always counted on to be there. It is something that has to be rebuilt every day, but hopefully to new heights each time. It is a place from which we leave behind our selfishness and pride—even if the loss of them is painful, and push on towards the greater things we can build together that are ahead.

Key #6
Above All Else, Beware of Selfishness;
It Is at The Root of Every Relationship Problem
You Will Ever Face

If there is anything that blinds more than the feelings of infatuation we call "falling in love," it is selfishness and its ability to justify almost anything. One of the miraculous benefits of marriage is that it saves us from ourselves—it saves us from lapsing into self-centeredness and self-justification and thereby doing things to hurt those around us because we can't see beyond our own selfish desires.

Committing yourself to performing acts of love is the only true cure for selfishness. Being loving because you feel loving is just manipulating the other person to give you what you want—in other words, "loving" them only so that you can get your needs and desires met. Acts of love, though, are seeds sown into her life that don't have any immediate benefit to you. You are just planting, tending, and protecting your garden so that it will be more beautiful and show you care. If you do so, someday you will get a return bigger than anything you could manipulate and squeeze out, and it will comeback of its own free will rather than through your conniving. It is the difference between taking the fruit of the tree of life with permission versus stealing it—one is the essence of life itself, the other a false sense of it—life is given, but it grows more hollow and emptier the more of it you steal.

Key #7
Effective Communication Starts with Listening. Only Work on Your Responses Once You Understand What She Is Really Saying

Too often couples talk across each other; each struggling to emphasize their point regardless of what the other is saying. Yet there is no communication without understanding, and while making a point is important, chances are that it will only be heard if you make it in a way that is relevant to what the other person just said.

~

Peace cannot be kept by force; it can only be achieved by understanding.
Albert Einstein

~

We need to remember that arguments in marriage should never be about which one is right as much as they are about resolving the issue at hand. Too often, however, we are not looking for resolution as much as we are exacting some kind of emotional victory over the other. Solving problems must be built on understanding in a win-win situation, not winning at the expense of the other's loss.

Key #8
Never Forget:
You Are on the Same Side

This key backs up the previous key in that anytime your wife loses, ultimately you do too, especially if you are the one who caused that loss. We need to realize that often the same things that drive us crazy about our spouse are the strengths she brings into the relationship that we don't have ourselves. When she just knows something and can't explain why, we can't let that infuriate our logic, but we need to accept it as her intuition about the matter at hand. When she says something about the way we speak to others or how we have treated someone, we need to recognize that she has seen something we did not and resist getting defensive about it.

Too often, however, personal hurts cloud our judgment and—like the old comic strip where the husband's boss yells at him, the husband yells at the wife, the wife yells at the kid, and the kid kicks the dog—the reason we snap at one person often has little to do with them. Thus the next key:

Key #9
When You Come to The End of Your Rope
Choose to Respond in Love And Forgiveness
It Is Your Only Chance to Get
What You Really Want

How many people who get divorces *really* want that? We never go into a marriage looking forward to the time when we are both so tapped out emotionally that we can't stand to live with the other person any more. This is one of the reasons that a man or woman who marries someone expecting that they will now feel satisfied and happy is in for such a let down. Yes, marriage certainly will make us happy, but it will also bottom us out. When it bottoms us out, and we have nothing other than our spouse to refill out emotional bank accounts, where do we get the energy to go on? If each partner does not have their own purposes to plug into and their own sense of who they are as an individual to give them stability, then all they will ever do to one another is make emotional withdrawals from each other until both are overdrawn.

Being the "less emotional" sex, however, means that we men are the ones who should be finding the strength to break the downward cycle of tapping each other out and deciding instead to forgive the past and perform acts of love to feed the future. Remember, you don't have to feel love to perform acts of love. There are times when you must choose to be a blessing even if she seems to be constantly doing the opposite towards you.

~

A successful marriage requires falling in love many times, always with the same person.
Mignon McLaughlin

~

It is a love that must act unselfishly because it can go long unreciprocated, especially if both parties are running on empty. In other words, it will take quite some time to get their "love tank" to overflowing again. We have to make the conscious choice to love regardless of feelings, otherwise we are liable to lose all we hoped for in getting married in the first place.

Key #10
In Marriage, The Golden Rule
—"Treat Others as You Want to Be Treated"—
does not work. You Need to Treat Her in The Way She Hears Love,
Not The Way You Hear It

Men, we need to recognize that buying our wives the latest, greatest ratchet set or a new deer hunting bow is probably not going to have the effect we are thinking it will (though, of course, I am sure there are exceptions to this!). We need to acknowledge that it is very unlikely our wives will hear love the way we do, so we need to go back to Wife U and enroll in "How Does She Hear Love 101." Watch her and see what things you do that really make her want to cuddle. When does she shine the happiest?

What excites her the most? What makes her smile? What makes her radiate more beauty? Learn these things and experiment with them to see what works best and stay out of the proverbial rut.

Stay creative in what you do. It doesn't have to cost you a bunch of money—even just calling her up in the middle of the day to tell her you are thinking of her will make a difference. Listen when you are out together to what she likes and plan your gifts months in advance. Sit and have a coffee with her and really listen. Help around the house or cover dinner a night or two a week. Surprise her as often as possible in ways that nurture her and make her more confident in your love and leadership.

Key #11
Your Wife Will Never Respect You as The Leader of Your Family Until You Give Her A Vision And A Man Worth Following

Too many of us spend more time planning the future of the businesses we don't even own than we do in planning the future of our families. We need to sow to the future and reap from the past. Whatever we give towards planning and providing for tomorrow will benefit us more in the long run than any temporary pleasure derived from spending our efforts and resources on fulfilling today's desires.

Regardless of whether you want the responsibility or not, you are the example for your family. If you are a man of truth and integrity, then all of your family members will reflect that—if you are not, they will reflect that as well. This doesn't mean you can never make mistakes, but in the important things like honesty, openness, affection, patience, balance, and the like, you need to lead the way.

Unfortunately, none of these traits and values really come naturally, especially if we had fathers who never showed them to us. As always, change starts with you. If you want a better family life than what you had growing up, then you will have to purpose and plan to break the natural cycle of simply following in your father's footsteps. If, however, you had a great dad as I did, then you need to think about what he did right and nurture the good attributes that he planted in you.

Not only do you need to have a vision, but you need to communicate it and let your family take ownership of it. Don't dictate it to them, but let it be a plan that you can discuss together and that will evolve as you grow as a couple. As your kids get old enough, let them participate as well. Family togetherness comes not only from playing together, but working together towards common goals. As much as you are working hard to provide for their activities, allowance, and college education, you should let them give back at least in the way of small chores or responsibilities that help the family.

Key #12
Your Wife Should Grow More Beautiful And Fulfilled Daily Because of Your Love And Nurturing

Your wife is a reflection of your love for her. She was gorgeous on your wedding day because it was her day to shine. You are the one who gave that to her. However, never let it be said of you that "The wedding was a success, but the marriage was a disaster!" Your wife should have more inner beauty shining from her after five years of marriage than she did on your wedding day; and even more on your tenth, twentieth, and fiftieth anniversaries! She may grow older on the outside, but it is up to you to keep her young on the inside.

∼

People say, "Relationships are made in heaven."
That may be true on some level, but relationships
are managed on earth.
Dr. Phil McGraw

∼

Help her plug into her own purpose and dreams and reach towards her own potential while also working together to reach for the goals and aspirations of your family. You not only hold the key to her heart, but also the key to her realizing who she can be. If you feed her hopes, she will feed yours and build your family's in the process. In the dance of life, you must lead, and the better a leader you are, the more she will shine.

LOVE LIKE A REAL MAN

While falling in love may blindside you like Cupid shooting you with an arrow, lasting love takes some forethought and real work. However, the rewards are also much greater. Instead of building your future on infatuation, you will be building it on a more solid and controllable love that can turn into a tremendous platform to propel you into a future of joy and fulfillment.

But in order for all of this to work, you have to take responsibility. You have to not only take the steering wheel, but make sure the car has gas, is running smoothly, shifted into the right gear, and the proper pressure is applied on the accelerator. In other words, you need to commit to making your marriage work, you have to plan ahead, make regular maintenance checks, and keep things moving forward even when there are bumps in the road. No one expects you to be perfect, especially those who love you, but they do expect you to be able to say those three magic phrases, "I was wrong," "I am sorry," and "Let's do it your way this time"—and as you know, "I love you," should be used as often as possible without losing its meaning.

Once again, though, I want you to realize that this does not mean taking a place of weakness in your marriage. Men who must be dictators are not stronger; they actually tend to be more insecure. You cannot confidently let you wife have her way if you are not also confident in your own manhood and that what you are doing is best for your family and yourself. If you always say "yes" to your wife even when you don't really agree with her just because you want to avoid a fight, then you have a completely different problem on your hand. In that case, you have some work to do on yourself before you can get back to working to build up your wife and your relationship.

However, I believe that no matter where you are in your relationship with your significant other—whether you have been dating and are contemplating popping the question—or the ink has yet to dry on your divorce papers—I know that these eleven keys can help you find a satisfying future. Start learning and applying them today.

Remember, the joy comes in the journey and working it through together. There is never a point where you can say, "Ah, now I have arrived," and rest on your laurels. However, if you do apply these principles, there will be rest and refreshment in your relationship together that will be like nothing you can find anywhere else in the world.

I wish you Godspeed in building your lasting love!

A PERSONAL NOTE

My purpose in writing this book was to share principles that I know work across cultures, ethnicities, faiths, and nationalities without any prejudice or bias. I hope I have accomplished this and that whatever your background you have found these principles to be as revolutionary as I have in my own life. However, with that said, I would also feel this book to be somewhat dishonest if I did not share one more important principle with you that has been my personal springboard for applying these keys in my own life.

Time and again in these pages I have emphasized that you need to find a place of purpose and strength from which to love your wife as she should be loved. For me, this strength has only come through a deeply spiritual and personal relationship with Jesus Christ as my Savior and Lord. My strength to forgive comes from the fact that He has forgiven me. My example to love without expecting anything in return has come from His example of how He loved and sacrificed for all of us. My hope that marriages can be rebuilt and that second or third marriages can work out where others have failed is wrapped up in the fact that after three days buried in the ground as dead, Jesus rose to new life and chose to raise us up with Him.

In John 10:10, Jesus said that He came that we might have "life . . . more abundantly." To this end, as a Christian and a pastor, I have set myself to study and help people live to their fullest both personally and in what I feel can be the closest we can come to heaven on earth in marriage.

If you lack direction, or the strength you know you need to live this kind of abundant life, I urge you to find a church in your area that teaches about Jesus in a way where you can meet Him personally and spiritually for yourself. If you do, it will not only give you a new lease on life, but give you the strength that you need to improve, and perhaps even repair, your relationships with your spouse and family members.

If this is your desire, then let it start with this simple prayer:

Lord Jesus,

I ask You to be the Lord of my life. I've made a mess out of things and I need Your help and I need Your forgiveness. From this day forward, I want to build on the right foundation, putting You first, trusting in You, and getting into Your Word, the Bible, so that it can be the food my spirit needs to love as You have shown how.

A Personal Note

From this day forward, I ask You to give me the strength to love my wife and family, present or future, as you have loved Your Church on the earth. Show me how to become a man like You were on earth, and be a blessing to everyone I meet.

I ask these things in Jesus' name, Amen.

BIBLIOGRAPHY

Chapman, Gary. The Five Love Languages: How to Express Heartfelt Commitment to Your Mate. Chicago: Northfield Publishing, 1992, 1995, 2004.

Commission on Children at Risk, The. Hardwired to Connect: The New Scientific Case for Authoritative Communities. New York: The Institute for American Values, 2003.

Gray, Ph.D.; John. Men Are from Mars, Women Are from Venus: The Classic Guide to Understanding the Opposite Sex. New York: Quill, 1992.

Rainy, Dennis and Barbara. Staying Close: Stopping the Natural Drift Toward Isolation in Marriage. Nashville: Thomas Nelson Books, 2003.